Alan Bennett first appeared on the stage in the revue *Beyond the Fringe*. His stage plays include *Forty Years On*, *Habeas Corpus*, *The Old Country*, *Enjoy*, *Kafka's Dick* and an adaptation of Kenneth Grahame's *The Wind in the Willows* for the National Theatre. He has also written many television plays, including *An Englishman Abroad* and a series of monologues, *Talking Heads*.

by the same author

plays

FORTY YEARS ON with GETTING ON,
HABEAS CORPUS and ENJOY
THE OLD COUNTRY
OFFICE SUITE
TWO KAFKA PLAYS
SINGLE SPIES
THE WIND IN THE WILLOWS

television

THE WRITER IN DISGUISE
OBJECTS OF AFFECTION (BBC)
TALKING HEADS (BBC)
POETRY IN MOTION (CHANNEL 4)

screenplays

A PRIVATE FUNCTION
PRICK UP YOUR IDEAS

autobiography

THE LADY IN THE VAN (LRB)

THE MADNESS
OF
GEORGE III

ALAN BENNETT

faber and faber
LONDON · BOSTON

First published in 1992
by Faber and Faber Limited
3 Queen Square London WC1N 3AU

Photoset by Parker Typesetting Service, Leicester
Printed by Clays Ltd, St Ives Plc

Alan Bennett is hereby identified as author of this work in accordance with
Section 77 of the Copyright, Designs and Patents Act 1988

All rights whatsoever in this play are strictly reserved and applications for
performance, etc., to The Peters Fraser & Dunlop Group Ltd, 503/4 The
Chambers, Chelsea Harbour, Lots Road, London SW10 0XF

A CIP record for this book is available from the British Library.
ISBN 0–571–16749–7

2 4 6 8 10 9 7 5 3

INTRODUCTION

I've always had a soft spot for George III, starting all of forty years ago when I was in the sixth form at Leeds Modern School and reading for a scholarship to Cambridge. The smart book around that time was Herbert Butterfield's *The Whig Interpretation of History*, which took the nineteenth century to task for writing history with one eye on the future, and in particular for taking as the only path through the past the development of democratic institutions. On the Whig interpretation historical characters got a tick if they were on the side of liberty (Cromwell, Chatham), a cross (Charles I, James II) if they held up the march of progress. Because he went in for active royalty and made some attempt to govern on his own account rather than leaving it to the Whig aristocracy, George III had been written up as a villain and a clumsy tyrant. This view Butterfield had helped to discredit, so a question on George III was thought likely to turn up in the Cambridge examination, which it duly did. Sitting in the freezing Senate House in December 1951 I trotted out my Butterfield and though I didn't get a scholarship, counted myself lucky to be offered a place at Sydney Sussex, that Christmas when the college letter came the best Christmas of my life.

Before university, though, there was National Service to be got through, regarded at best as a bore but for me, as a late developer, a long-dreaded ordeal; it was touch and go which I got to first – puberty or the call-up. I served briefly in the infantry then like many university entrants at that time was sent on the Joint Services Language Course to learn Russian, firstly at Coulsdon, then at Cambridge. So what I had dreaded turned out a happy time and, though I didn't realize it then, far more enjoyable than my time at university proper. However, I began to think that since I was now spending a year at Cambridge studying Russian the gilt was off the gingerbread so far as Cambridge was concerned and I might get the best of both worlds if I were to go to Oxford. This wasn't altogether the beady-eyed career move it might seem, in that I had a hopeless crush on one of my fellow officer cadets, who was bound for Oxford (that his college was Brasenose, then a mecca for rowing and rugger, somehow exemplifying the utter futility of it). Still, I suppose I ought to have been grateful; he might have been going to Hull – or even to Leeds.

So now in the evenings, after we'd finished our Russian lessons, I started to work for a scholarship again, biking in along Trumpington Road to work in the Cambridge Reference Library, a dark Victorian building behind the Town Hall (and gaslit in memory, though it surely can't have been). George III was about to make his second entrance. Sometime that autumn I bought, at Deighton Bell in Trinity Street, a copy of *George III and the Politicians* by Richard Pares, a book I have still, my name written in it by a friend, as I disliked my handwriting then as I do now. It was a detailed, allusive book, demanding a more thorough knowledge of eighteenth-century politics than a schoolboy could be expected to have, but I mugged it up. Like the good examinee I always was I realized that to know one book well is a better bet than having a smattering of several. A year in the army had made me more flash too, so this time I did get a scholarship, to read history at Exeter College, where I went when I came out of the army six months later.

The Oxford history syllabus takes in the whole of English history, beginning at the Beginnings and finishing in those days at 1939. This meant that one didn't get round to the eighteenth century until the middle of the final year. Seeing that Pares, of whom I knew nothing other than his book, was lecturing at Rhodes House, I went along, to find it only sparsely attended, though curiously for a general lecture I saw that quite a few of the audience were dons.

When Pares was brought in it was immediately plain why. Propped up in a wheelchair, nodding, helpless and completely paralysed, he was clearly dying. Someone spread his notes out on a board laid across his knees and he began to lecture, his head sunk on his chest but his voice still strong and clear. It was noticeable even in the eight weeks that I attended his lectures that the paralysis was progressive and that he was getting weaker, and

I fancy that in the final weeks as he was unable to turn his head someone sat beside him to move his notes into his line of vision.

Now, the eighteenth century is not an inspiring period. Whether by the Whig interpretation or not, there are none of those great constitutional struggles and movements of ideas that animate the seventeenth and dramatize the nineteenth. The politics are materialistic, small-minded, the House of Commons an arena where a man might make a name for himself but where most members were just concerned to line their pockets. That Pares, with death at his elbow, should have gone on analysing and lecturing on what I saw as such a thankless time made a great impression on me, the lesson put crudely, I suppose, that if a thing is not worth doing, it's worth doing well. As it was, these must have been the last lectures Pares gave – he died the following year – but when I found I was able to stay on after taking my degree to do research and teach a little and possibly become a don, the memory of those lectures cast for me a romantic light on what is a pretty unromantic profession.

Pares kept cropping up in subsequent years. As the memoirs and letters of the twenties began to be published it turned out that as an undergraduate he had been one of the group round Evelyn Waugh and Harold Acton. But whereas most of that charmed circle went down without taking a degree, Pares turned his back on all that, took a First in Greats and was elected a Fellow of All Souls. Thirty years later, in December 1954, Evelyn Waugh wrote to Nancy Mitford: 'I went up to Oxford and visited my first homosexual love, Richard Pares, a don at All Souls. At 50 he is quite paralysed except his mind and voice, awaiting deterioration and death. A wife and four daughters, no private fortune. He would have been Master of Balliol if he had not been struck down. No Christian faith to support him. A very harrowing visit.'

My vision of myself pursuing an academic career did not last long, though as a postgraduate I was supervised by the medieval historian K. B. McFarlane, who had, incidentally, shared a flat with Pares when they were both drafted into the Civil Service during the war. McFarlane was a great teacher and yet he scarcely seemed to teach at all. An hour with him and though he barely touched on the topic of my research, I would come away thinking

vii

that to study medieval history was the only thing in the world worth doing. McFarlane himself had no such illusions, once referring to medieval studies as 'just a branch of the entertainment business', though when with the onset of *Beyond the Fringe* I eventually abandoned medieval studies for the entertainment business this did not make him any less displeased. The rest, one would like to say, is history. But of course what it had been was history; what it was to be was not history at all and when I began to read for this present play a couple of years ago, it was the first systematic historical work I'd done in twenty years.

In the meantime I found that George III's rehabilitation had proceeded apace. No longer the ogre, he had grown altogether more kindly, wiser even, and in his attachment to his people and his vision of the nation over and above the vagaries of politics he had come to seem a forerunner of a monarch of the present day. But it was a joke that made me think of writing about him – just as when a few years ago I thought of writing about Kafka, what started me off was a joke that Kafka had made on his deathbed. Dying of tuberculosis of the larynx, he was fetching up a good deal of phlegm. 'I think,' he said (and the joke is more poignant for being so physically painful to make), 'I think I deserve the Nobel Prize for sputum.' Nothing if not sick, it is a joke that could have been made yesterday. Less poignant, George III's joke also occurred during his illness. He had an equerry, Colonel Manners, who, bringing him his dinner one day, discovered the King had hidden under the sofa. A Jeeves before his time, Manners imperturbably laid a place for His Majesty on the carpet and put down the plate. He was retiring discreetly when the King said (still *sous bergère*), 'That was very good . . . Manners,' the pun thought to signal a further stage in the King's recovery. The anecdote hasn't found its way into the play but it did make me think that George III might be fun to write about.

My interest in the King's story had also been rekindled by reading some of the medical history that was being published in the 1980s, particularly by Roy Porter. Michael Neve and Jonathan Miller separately suggested that the madness of George III would make a play, and Neve lent me *The Royal Malady* by Charles Chenevix Trench, which is still the best account of the

King's illness and the so-called Regency Crisis. I also read *George III and the Mad Business* by the mother-and-son partnership Richard Hunter and Ida Macalpine, who first put forward the theory that the King's illness was physical not mental and that he was suffering from porphyria. I found it a difficult book to read, convincing about George III himself but less so about the other historical cases the authors identified, the slightest regal indisposition seized on to fetch the sufferer under porphyria's umbrella.

From a dramatist's point of view it is obviously useful if the King's malady was a toxic condition, traceable to a metabolic disturbance rather than due to schizophrenia or manic depression. Thus afflicted, he becomes the victim of his doctors and a tragic hero. How sympathetic this would make him to the audience I had not realized until the previews of the play. I had been worried that the climax came two thirds of the way into the second act, when the King begins to recover, and that there was no real dramatic development after that. What I had not anticipated was that the audience would be so whole-heartedly on the King's side, or that when he does recover it would prove such a relief of tension that the rest of the play, in which little happens except that various loose ends are tied up, goes by on a wave of delighted laughter. 'The King is himself again' means that the audience can once more take pleasure in his eccentricities, enjoy the discomfiture of the doctors until in a nice sentimental conclusion Mr and Mrs King are united in regal domesticity.

Having been working on the play for a year or so I had eventually by April 1991 got it into some sort of order, when, knowing it was far from finished and in some despair, I put it through Nicholas Hytner's door. Coming away from the house I felt rather like one of those practical jokers who arrange for an unsuspecting victim to be landed with a load of slurry. That Hytner was then enthusiastic about the script and with him the director of the National Theatre, Richard Eyre, cheered me so much that I forced myself to re-read it. No, I had been right; slurry at that moment it was. Later I discovered that Hytner had a gap in his schedule and Richard Eyre a gap in his, so that the script had come as the answer to both their prayers.

Reading the play for the first time and knowing only a little of the period Nicholas Hytner had been surprised when the King recovered. With this in mind his first suggestion was that I should make the play more of a cliffhanger, relying on the fact that most people would know there was a Regency without quite knowing when it began, or that the Prince of Wales would have to wait another twenty years before he finally got his hands on the government. This was just the first of many invaluable suggestions he made and in the course of the next three months the play was completely reshaped. The role of a director at this stage of a play is more like that of an editor and, as other dramatists will testify, the directors who can fill this role are few and far between. I count myself lucky to have found such a collaborator.

Though it began and ended much as it did in the finished version, the original manuscript meandered about quite a bit, so the two rewritings I did between April and August cut out a good deal in an effort to make the progress of the King's illness and his recovery more clear. In August 1991 a reading of the text was set up in the National Theatre Studio, actors working at the National taking the various parts almost on a first-come-first-served basis, the purpose being for us to hear the text and see how it played. The only actor already cast was Nigel Hawthorne and it was plain from his reading how he would transform the part. That said, to sit and hear the play read, knowing it was unfinished, was both depressing and embarrassing, and I fear that some of the actors, who seldom see a play at this stage, must have wondered why we were bothering. However I then began a third rewrite which solved many of the problems the reading had thrown up and gave the play more dramatic thrust; this was the script we began to rehearse at the end of September.

That we were able to rehearse for ten weeks was a great luxury, and one possible only in a subsidized company. However, in that time Nicholas Hytner had also to rehearse the new production of *The Wind in the Willows*, so it was Pitt and Fox in the morning, Rat and Mole (and Fox) in the afternoon. When at the end of the seventh week we were able to run the play, it was immediately clear that while the course of the King's illness and recovery was plain and worked dramatically, the political crisis it brought with it lacked urgency. So the final bout of rewriting was only a couple of weeks before the play went on stage. I have never worked on a play where so much reconstruction has been required. That it was unresented by the actors, who by this stage in rehearsal are naturally anxious for a finished text, says a good deal both for their forbearance and for the atmosphere in which the rehearsals were conducted. Not since *Forty Years On*, which is, I suppose, my only other historical play, have I enjoyed rehearsals so much.

One casualty of the rewrites was strict historical truth. In the early versions of the play I had adhered pretty closely to the facts: the Prince of Wales, for instance, was originally a more genial character than presented here and more reluctant to have it admitted in public or in the press that his father might be mad. However the play works only if the antipathy between father and son, never far below the surface with all the Hanoverian kings, is sharpened and the Prince made less sympathetic. In the original Fox, too, was a more ambiguous character and much troubled by his own lack of scruple, and the votes in the Commons were not so narrow, the Government majority never as low as ten. In other respects, though, events needed no sharpening, the King's recovery for instance being only slightly less dramatic than it is in the play; certainly it took the politicians by surprise. This was because the King's illness was such a political football that no one was quite sure what information was to be trusted, and even when the King was plainly on the mend the doctors could not guarantee that he would maintain the improvement (and there were some alarming lapses).

In this process of recovery the 'what-whatting' was crucial. This verbal habit of the King's was presumably the attempt of a nervous and self-conscious man to prevent the conversation from flagging, always a danger in chats with the monarch as the subject is never certain whether he or she is expected to reply or when. The onset of the King's mania delivered him from self-consciousness and so the 'what-whatting' went; the King was in any case talking too fast and too continuously for there to be need or room for it. When he began to calm down and come to himself again he came to the 'what-whatting' too, the flag of social distress now a signal of recovery. As Greville wrote, 'though not a grace in language, yet the restoring habits of former days prescribed a forerunner of returning wisdom.'

I have no experience of royal persons, some of whom I think may still 'what-what' a little. Today, though, it's easier. What royalty wants nowadays is deference without awe, though what they get more often than not is a fatuous smile, any social awkwardness veiled in nervous laughter, so that the Queen moves among her people buoyed up on waves of obliging hilarity. How happy we must all seem! Such tittering would have been unthinkable at the court of George III, reputedly the dullest in Europe, where no one laughed or coughed and where it was unthinkable ever to sneeze.

Had the King insisted on such formality outside the court he would not have been as popular as he was. A stickler for etiquette at home, he and the Queen remained seated while his courtiers stood for hours at a time, drooping with boredom, but outside the court, often riding unattended, he would stop and chat with farm labourers, road-menders and anybody he came across. When they went to Cheltenham he promised the Queen, with a lack of formality that not so long ago was thought to be a modern breakthrough, that they would 'walk about and meet his subjects'.

One difficulty when writing the play was how to furnish the audience with sufficient information about the political set-up at the end of the eighteenth century for them to understand why the illness of the King threatened the survival of the Government. Nowadays of course it wouldn't, and the fact that there were seemingly two parties, Tories and Whigs, could mislead an audience into thinking that then and nowadays were much the same.

What has to be understood is that in 1788 the monarch was still the engine of the nation. The King would choose as his chief minister a politician who could muster enough support in the House of Commons to give him a majority. Today it is the other way round: the majority in the Commons determines the choice of prime minister. Though it sometimes seemed like this even in the eighteenth century, a minister imposed on the King by Parliament could not last long; this was why George III so much resented Fox, who was briefly his minister following a disreputable coalition with North in 1783. All governments were

xii

to some degree coalitions and a majority in the Commons did not reflect some overall victory by Whigs or Tories in a general election. Leading figures in Parliament had their groups of supporters; there were Pitt-ites, Fox-ites, Rockingham Whigs and Grenvilles, who voted as their patron voted. A ministry was put together, a majority accumulated out of an alliance of various groups, and what maintained that alliance was the uninterrupted flow of political patronage, the network of offices and appointments available to those running the administration. In the play Sir Boothby Skrymshir and his nephew Ramsden are a ridiculous pair, but as Sheridan says (though the phrase was actually used by Fox), they are the 'marketable flotsam' out of which a majority was constructed. At the head of the pyramid was the King. All appointments flowed from him. If he was incapacitated and his powers transferred to his son, support for the ministry would dwindle because the flow of patronage had stopped. If the King was mad it would not be long before the Ins were Out.

As I struggled to mince these chunks of information into credible morsels of dialogue (the danger always being that characters are telling each other what they know *in their bones*), I often felt it would have been simpler to call the audience in a quarter of an hour early and give them a short curtain lecture on the nature of eighteenth-century politics before getting on with the play proper.

The characters are largely historical. Margaret Nicholson's attempt on the King's life was in 1786, not just before his illness as in the play, but it is certainly true, as the King remarks, that in France she would not have got off so lightly. As it was, she lived on in Bedlam long after all the witnesses to her deed were dead, surviving until the eve of the accession of George III's grand-daughter, Queen Victoria.

I thought I had invented Fitzroy but discover that in 1801 George III had an aide-de-camp of this name, who was later the heart-throb of the King's youngest daughter, Amelia. He was 'generally admitted to be good-looking in a rather wooden sort of way, he had neither dash nor charm and seems to have been on the frigid side into the bargain', which describes our Fitzroy exactly. That he was playing a double game and was an intimate of the Prince of Wales is my invention.

Greville is an historical character, his diary one of the most important sources for the history of the royal malady. However, Greville was not in attendance throughout as he is in the play. A fair-minded though conventional man, and clear-sighted where the King's illness was concerned (and often appalled at its treatment), Greville along with the King's other attendants was excluded when Dr Willis took on the case. Willis brought with him some of his own staff, presumably from his asylum at Greatham in Lincolnshire, and took on other heavies in London. In the play they appear only once, when the restraining chair is brought in at the end of the first act, but in fact they remained at Windsor and Kew in constant attendance on the King until Willis eventually went back north. This was not, as in the play, immediately before the thanksgiving service in June 1789, but some months later.

The number of physicians attending the King varied. They were known as the 'London doctors' to distinguish them from Dr Willis and his son. I have restricted them to three but there may have been as many as ten. Nor have I included Willis's son, who was also a doctor and subsequently in charge of the King during his next attack in 1802.

The pages who in the play bear so much of the burden of the King's illness were probably older than I have made them, the youngest and kindest, Papandiek, being the King's barber, with his wife another of those who kept a diary of this much journalized episode. Some pages were sacked when the King recovered because 'from the manner in which they had been obliged to attend on Him during the illness, they had obtained a sort of familiarity which now would not be pleasing to Him.' However, these were not Papandiek and Braun. In the play depicted as a heartless creature, Braun was in fact one of the King's favourites and still in his service ten years later. The other page, Fortnum, did, as is said, leave to found the grocer's and in the seventies, I remember, one used to be accosted in the store in far-from-eighteenth-century language by two bewigged figures, Mr Fortnum and Mr Mason, who were actually two unemployed actors.

I found the Opposition (an anachronistic phrase for which there is no convenient substitute) much harder to write than the Government. 'What can they *do*?' Nicholas Hytner would ask, which is the same question of course that opposition politicians are always having to ask themselves, even today. Pitt, Dundas and Thurlow carry on the government; Fox, Sheridan and Burke can only talk about the day when they might have the government to carry on. And drink, of course. But, as the King says, 'they all drink.' Pitt was frequently drunk before a big speech and on one occasion was sick behind the Speaker's chair.

With Pitt I had first to rid myself of the picture I retained of him from childhood when I saw Korda's wartime propaganda film *The Young Mr Pitt*. Robert Donat was Pitt, kitted out with a kindly housekeeper, adoring chums and maybe even a girlfriend. What there was no sign of was the bottle. At one point in the play he talks of when he was a boy, though boy he never really was, brought up by his father to be prime minister, destined always for 'the first employments'. The son, the nephew and the first cousin of prime ministers, the only commoner in a cabinet of peers, perhaps he was arrogant but no wonder. Long, lank and awkward, he made a wonderful caricature, and if he was the first prime minister in the sense we understand it today it was because the cartoonists made him so.

Pitt's career ran in tandem with that of Fox, though Fox was the older man. Meeting the boy Pitt he seems to have had a premonition that here was his destiny. They are such inveterate and complementary opposites, Pitt cold, distant and calculating, Fox warm, convivial and impulsive, that they are almost archetypes, save or squander, hoard or spend, Gladstone and Disraeli, Robespierre and Danton, Eliot and Pound. Pitt had his disciples but Fox, for all his inconsistencies and political folly, was genuinely loved, even by his opponents (though never by the King). His oratory was spellbinding, as Pitt ruefully acknowledged ('Ah,' he said to one of Fox's critics, 'but you have never been under the wand of the magician.'). Burke, whom posterity remembers as a great orator, was in his day considered a bore, his speeches often ludicrously over the top, and known as 'the dinner bell' because when he rose to speak he regularly emptied the House.

Fox had charm, even at his lowest ebb. 'I have led a sad life,' he wrote to his mistress, 'sitting up late, always either at the House of Commons or gaming, and losing my money every night that I have played. Getting up late, of course and finding people in my room so that I have never had the morning time to myself, and have gone out as soon as I could, though generally very late, to get rid of them, so that I have scarce ever had a moment to write. You have heard how poor a figure we made in numbers on the slave trade, but I spoke I believe very well . . . and it is a cause in which one cannnot help being pleased with oneself for having done right.' Baffled as to how to convey Fox's charm, I included much of this letter in the first draft of the play, the speech originally part of the much altered final scene. 'A danger this is becoming Fox's story,' noted Nicholas Hytner, so I took it out again.

I made Sheridan a man of business, a manager of the House, and he was certainly more canny than Fox, whom he regularly scolded and who, he always said, treated him as if he were a swindler. I began by peppering his speeches with self-quotation, which is never a wise move. I had done the same with Orton in an early draft of the screenplay of *Prick Up Your Ears*, and that didn't work either; one thinks too of all the movies about Wilde in which he talks in epigrams throughout. There was originally a parody of the screen scene in *School for Scandal*, in which the Prince of Wales and his doctor are discovered hiding from the King. It had some basis in fact but it was an early casualty. I give him two shots at explaining it but what I find hard to understand is why, having made a name for himself in the theatre, Sheridan should have wanted to go into politics at all. On the rare occasions I have talked to politicians, I have found myself condescended to because I'm not 'in the know' (political journalists and civil servants do it too). So perhaps that was part of it. Poor Sheridan never quite managed to be one of the boys, even in death. In Westminster Abbey Pitt, Fox and Burke are buried clubbily together, whereas Sheridan has landed up next to Garrick. His distaste for this location was another casualty of the final scene of the play. Of course what I really wanted to include but daren't was the playwright's bane, a conversation (with Thurlow, it would be) beginning, 'Anything in the pipeline, Sheridan?'

Dundas was much older than I have made him but, dramatically, Pitt needs a friend or else he would never unburden himself at all. Thurlow, foul-tongued and 'lazy as a toad at the bottom of a well', was well known to be a twister. When he made the speech on the King's recovery, quoted in the play – 'And when I forget my sovereign, may God forget me' – Wilkes, who was seated on the steps of the throne, remarked: 'God forget you? He'll see you damned first!'

Queen Charlotte was every bit as homely and parsimonious as she's presented, stamping the leftover pats of butter with her signet so that they would not be eaten by the servants. Her name is preserved in Apple Charlotte, a recipe that uses up stale bread. I thought I had caught her rather well until Janet Dale, who was playing her, said that the game little wife was a part to which she was no stranger: not long ago it was the first Mrs Orwell and more recently Mrs Walesa; 'Have another cup of tea, Lech, and let Solidarity take care of itself . . . Solidarity, *Animal Farm* or porphyria, I'm always the plucky little woman married to a hubby with problems.'

There are some fortuitous parallels with contemporary politics; and had the play been written before the downfall of Mrs Thatcher there would have been more. Pitt's 'kitchen principles' were not dissimilar to hers and one could see that Dundas having Willis redraft the bulletin while Pitt keep his hands clean is reminiscent of Mrs Thatcher's conduct in the Westland affair. Nor was Pitt's attitude to the arts unlike hers: 'Neither Porson as a scholar, nor Gibbon as an historian, nor Johnson as a lexicographer obtains a farthing from public funds. To Pitt literature, like linen and steel, is a commodity, the price of which must be fixed by supply and demand.' Thinking that the Regency Bill must pass and that he faces imminent dismissal, Pitt says that he needs five more years. The audience laughs. But what politician doesn't? Pitt of course got them, but what he actually meant was five more years of peace, and these he didn't get. Mrs Thatcher's fortunes were made by a war that came just in time, Pitt's ruined by a war which (as Fox thought) should not have come at all. The audience applauds again when Pitt, reviewing his seemingly bleak future, says that having been prime minister he does not now intend to sit on the back benches and carp. This isn't an easy gibe at Mr Heath, for whom I've got some sympathy; Pitt had always aspired to be prime minister, but on his own terms; in 1783 he had even refused the King an invitation to form a ministry because he was not yet ready; defeated, he would never have played second fiddle to anybody. Any account of politics whatever the period must throw up contemporary parallels. I think if I had deliberately made more of these it would have satisfied or pandered to some critics who felt that was what the play should have been more about. But it is about the madness of George III, the rest amusing, intriguing, but incidental. Mention of the critics, though, reminds me that one of the jokes when we were rehearsing the play was that it would take the audience ten minutes to reconcile themselves to the fact that it wasn't set in Halifax. Such jokes tempt fate and I'm told that the critic of the *Independent* spent most of his notice regretting that it wasn't more Trouble-at-t'-Mill.

Though I have known sufferers from severe depression, I have had little experience of mental illness or of the discourse of the mentally ill, since depression, though it can lead to delusions, doesn't disorder speech. Of course, as Greville cautions Willis in the play, the King's discourse is slightly disordered to begin with, not normal anyway, and his idiosyncratic utterance has to be established in the audience's mind before it gets more hurried and compulsive and he starts to go off the rails. Even then Willis has to tread warily because behaviour which in an ordinary person would be considered unbalanced (talking of oneself in the third person for instance) is perfectly proper in the monarch. Some of the contents of the King's mad speech I cribbed from contemporary sources, such as John Haslam's *Illustrations of Madness*, an account of James Tilly Matthews, a patient in Bethlem Hospital in 1810. Other features of the King's mad talk, his elaborate circumlocutions (a chair 'an article for sitting in', for instance), are characteristic of schizophrenic speech.

What was plain quite early on was that where mad talk was concerned a little went a long way; that while it is interesting to see the King going mad and a great relief to see him recover, when he is completely mad and not making any sense at all he is of no dramatic consequence. Since what he is saying is irrational it cannot affect the outcome of things, and so is likely to be ignored; thus an audience will attend to what is being done to the King but not to what he is saying. There was also a difficulty with the sheer quantity of the King's discourse (on one occasion he was reported as talking continuously for nine hours at a stretch). Two minutes' drivel, however felicitously phrased, is enough to make an audience restive, and though what the King is saying is never quite drivel, the volume of it has to be taken down to allow other characters to speak across him, subject sense taking precedence over regal nonsense. Of course speech is not the half of it, and without Nigel Hawthorne's transcendent performance the King could have been just a gabbling bore and his fate a matter of indifference. As it is, the performance made him such a human and sympathetic figure the audience saw the whole play through his eyes.

The final scene of the play proved the most difficult to get right. I knew from the start that the play must end at St Paul's when the nation gives thanks for the King's return to health. As originally written the doctors emerged still quarrelling as to who deserves the credit for their patient's recovery. Then Dr Richard Hunter, the joint-author of *George III and the Mad Business*, materialized in modern dress to tell the eighteenth-century doctors that they were all wrong anyway and that the King was not mad but suffering from porphyria. The discussion that followed was long and detailed, too much so for this stage of the play and made longer when the politicians emerged and started quarrelling too. Finally the King himself came out, found the doctors disagreeing over the body of the patient, and the politicians disagreeing over the body of the state, said to hell with it all and, taking his cue from Hunter's futurity, described how he would eventually end up mad anyway.

Nigel Hawthorne felt, I think rightly, that he couldn't step out of his character so easily and that if he did the audience would feel cheated. It was Roy Porter who suggested that Richard Hunter's mother Ida Macalpine was as much responsible for *George III and the Mad Business* as her son and that in the interests of literary justice (and political correctness) she should be the voice of modern medicine. Accordingly I wrote the brief scene just before the finale where she explains to the sacked pages (who had been the only ones to take notice of the King's blue piss) what this symptom meant. Whereas in a film one could deal with this explanation in the final credits I felt at the time the play opened the facts had to be set out and the matter settled within the play. Now I'm less sure, though the scene has a structural function as it enables the King and Queen to nip out of bed and into their togs ready for the finale.

One ending I was fond of, though it was determinedly untheatrical, and perhaps just an elaborate way of saying that too many cooks spoil the broth; still, it's the nearest I can get to extracting a message from the play. The King and Queen are left alone on the stage after the Thanksgiving Service and they sit down on the steps of St Paul's and try and decide what lessons can be drawn from it all:

KING: The real lesson, if I may say so, is that what makes an illness perilous is celebrity. Or, as in my case, royalty. In the ordinary course of things doctors want their patients to recover; their reputations depend on it. But if the patient is rich or royal, powerful or famous, other considerations enter in. There are many parties interested apart from the interested party. So more doctors are called in and none but the best will do. But the best aren't always very good and they argue, they disagree. They have to because they are after all the best and the world is watching. And who is in the middle? The patient. It happened to me. It happened to Napoleon. It happened to Anthony Eden. It happened to the Shah. The doctors even killed off George V to make the first edition of *The Times*. I tell you, dear people, if you're poorly it's safer to be poor and ordinary.

QUEEN: But not too poor, Mr King.

KING: Oh no. Not too poor. What? What?

When I was writing the play I had no notion of how it could be put on except that I knew there was a flight of stairs at the rear of the stage. I saw the King and court coming rapidly into view at the start, then hastening down the stairs towards the front of the stage where there was an attempted assassination . . . an opening that may have been suggested by the line-up of the cast at the start of Richard Jones's production of *Too Clever By Half*. I could see the end too, a descent of the same stairs after the Service of Thanksgiving in St Paul's. How to stage the succession of scenes in between, scenes that were more like a script for a film than a play, I had no idea.

Mark Thompson's solution was a flight of steps that ran the full width of the stage at the rear, in front of them a panelled wall with two doors that could either be flown in as one piece or slid on in two halves from the wings. In addition, wires spanned the stage on which were two sets of light curtains. These could be drawn across the stage to reveal one area while screening another and thus a scene could be set up behind the curtain while another was played in front of it, the scene change then simply a question of the curtain being pulled across, generally by one of the cast. Though this arrangement is invariably described as 'Brechtian' by critics ('Brechtian' nowadays as two-edged a compliment as 'Shavian'), I can imagine no better solution. It minimized the time spent on scene changes which with any more cumbersome arrangement would have added twenty minutes to the play.

It will be obvious from this Introduction how much I owe to Nicholas Hytner. I would also like to thank the National Theatre staff director, Edward Kemp, the cast and production team, Anne Davies, Mary-Kay Wilmers and, for assistance with medical matters, Jonathan Miller, Roy Porter and Michael Neve.

Alan Bennett, December 1991

The Madness of George III was first performed at the Royal
National Theatre, London, on 28 November 1991. The cast
included:

GEORGE III	Nigel Hawthorne
QUEEN CHARLOTTE	Janet Dale
PRINCE OF WALES	Michael Fitzgerald
DUKE OF YORK	Mark Lockyer
PITT	Julian Wadham
DUNDAS	Patrick Pearson
THURLOW	James Villiers
FOX	David Henry
SHERIDAN	Iain Mitchell
BURKE	Peter Laird
MRS ARMISTEAD/	
DR IDA MACALPINE	Celestine Randall
FITZROY	Anthony Calf
GREVILLE	Daniel Flynn
LADY PEMBROKE/	
MARGARET NICHOLSON	Richenda Carey
PAPANDIEK	Matthew Lloyd Davies
FORTNUM	Brian Shelley
BRAUN	Paul Corrigan
SIR GEORGE BAKER	Harold Innocent
DR RICHARD WARREN	Jeremy Child
SIR LUCAS PEPYS	Cyril Shaps
DR WILLIS	Charles Kay
SIR BOOTHBY SKRYMSHIR	Mike Burnside
RAMSDEN	Paul Kynman
SIR SELBY MARKHAM	Alan Brown
HOPPNER	Nick Sampson

Director	Nicholas Hytner
Designer	Mark Thompson
Lighting	Paul Pyant
Music	Kevin Leeman
Sound	Scott Myers
Costume Supervisor	Irene Bohan

PART 1

WINDSOR

The curtain rises to Handel's Music for the Royal Fireworks, *the stage bare except for a flight of stairs. This spans the breadth of the stage and at the head of it, their backs to the audience, stand four* PAGES. *There is a shout off-stage from the* EQUERRIES:

Sharp! Sharp! The King! The King!

and the PAGES *come rapidly backwards down the steps as the* KING *and court climb the steep ramp at the rear of the staircase, so coming gradually into view. The* KING *and* QUEEN *pause briefly at the top, then come down the steps at a brisk pace, the pace as always set by the* KING. GEORGE III *is accompanied by his wife* QUEEN CHARLOTTE, *his son and heir the* PRINCE OF WALES *and his younger son the* DUKE OF YORK. *Flanking them are members of the government,* PITT, DUNDAS *and the Lord Chancellor,* THURLOW.

As the KING *reaches the foot of the stairs* MARGARET NICHOLSON, *a soberly dressed woman, comes forward with a petition and kneels to await the* KING. *He halts the procession, takes the petition, whereupon, as the music hits a grinding discord,* NICHOLSON *strikes him.*

KING: What? What? Hey, madam, what's this?

> (*The* KING *falls back, and there is a moment of shocked silence, then turmoil.*)

EQUERRIES: Back! Back! Hold her! Is Your Majesty hurt?

QUEEN: Sir! Sir!

KING: What, what? No no, I am not hurt.

> (FITZROY, *an equerry, and the* PAGES *struggle to restrain* NICHOLSON *as the* KING *is helped to his feet.*)

NICHOLSON: I have a property due to me from the Crown of England.

KING: The poor creature's mad. Do not hurt her, she's not hurt me.

NICHOLSON: Give me my property or the country will be drenched in blood.

KING: Will it indeed? Well, not with this, madam. It's a dessert knife. Wouldn't cut a cabbage.

I

NICHOLSON: I have a property due to me from the Crown of
England.

KING: Quite so, quite so.

(NICHOLSON *is hustled away*.)

QUEEN: You murderous fiend! (*Embracing* KING) Thank God I
have you yet.

KING: Hey, hey! Do not fuss, madam. The King has no wound,
just a torn waistcoat.

PRINCE OF WALES: One would consider that almost as vexing.

KING: What's that?

PRINCE OF WALES: I rejoice, papa, that you are unharmed.

QUEEN: The son rejoices. The Prince of Wales rejoices. Faugh!

DUKE OF YORK: Me too, pa. God save the King and so on.

QUEEN: (*Embracing him but looking at the* PRINCE OF WALES) And
he is fatter. Always fatter.

KING: Fatter because he is not doing, what, what? Do you know
England, sir?

PRINCE OF WALES: I think so, sir.

KING: You know Brighton, Bath – yes, but do you know its mills
and manufactories? Do you know its farms? Because I do.

(*There are subdued groans from the two brothers, who have had
this lecture before.*)

I have made them my special study. I've written pamphlets
on agriculture.

DUKE OF YORK: Yes, sir.

KING: Pigs, what.

PRINCE OF WALES: Yes, father.

KING: Stock. Good husbandry. Do you know what they call me?

PRINCE OF WALES: What do they call you, father?

KING: Farmer George. And do you know what that is?

PRINCE OF WALES: Impertinence?

KING: No, sir. Love.

QUEEN: Affection.

KING: It is admiration, sir.

QUEEN: Respect.

KING: What are your hobbies, sir?

PRINCE OF WALES: Hobbies?

QUEEN: Fashion.

KING: Furniture. Do you know what mine are? Learning. Astronomy.

QUEEN: The heavens are at his fingertips.

KING: It is not good, sir, this idleness. That is why you are fat. Do not be fat, sir. Fight it! Fight it!

(For a moment the Royal Family puts on an appearance of unity as the church bells are rung to celebrate the KING's deliverance, and the KING acknowledges the crowds. Then the PRINCE and the DUKE are waved away and the KING turns to WILLIAM PITT, a long, unbending figure in early middle age.)

You have had a lucky escape, Mr Pitt.

PITT: I, Your Majesty?

KING: Yes, you. What, what. You're my Prime Minister. I chose you. Anything happens to me you'll be out, what, what, and Mr Fox will be in. Hey, hey.

PITT: I think there's no danger of that, sir.

(THURLOW, having been left in charge of the would-be assassin, now returns, as do the PAGES, bringing a clean waistcoat.)

THURLOW: Your Majesty, the woman will be examined by the Privy Council. And if she is mad she will be confined in Bethlem Hospital.

KING: She is fortunate to live in this kingdom, hey? It is not long since a madman tried to stab the King of France. The wretch was subjected to the most fiendish torments – his limbs burned with fire, the flesh lacerated with red-hot pincers, until in a merciful conclusion, he was stretched between four horses and torn asunder.

(The KING is being helped off with his coat and as he raises his arms to enable the PAGES to undress him he too is outstretched. For a moment he seems to find it difficult to speak, as if he also is tortured (as indeed he will be). This uneasy moment is noted by the company and by the KING himself, but it passes and he is straightaway himself again.)

We have at least outgrown such barbarities. The lowliest subject in this kingdom could not be subjected to such tortures in the name of justice.

The church bells are still ringing as the stage clears and and FOX,
BURKE *and* SHERIDAN *come down the stairs.*

FOX: What has happened to this country? A despot escapes the
knife and they ring the bells.

BURKE: No, I do not believe that even Charles James Fox wants
the King killed.

FOX: I do not want anyone killed, but Burke my dear, to see him
dead, or removed – nothing would suit me better.

BURKE: No, not removed. Curbed perhaps. Circumscribed. The
monarch restrained. But not removed.

SHERIDAN: Well, he's not going to die. Someone who only drinks
barley-water? He'll outlive us all and with Pitt as his minister
we shall none of us have a whiff of government for five years.

FOX: Five? More like ten. And there is no way around him,
Sheridan. There is a fountain of ability in this nation, a clear
spring of good feeling and selfless endeavour, and blocking it
and polluting is George Rex. And Mr Pitt.

BURKE: And he was a Whig once, Pitt. Such promise!

SHERIDAN: We are all Whigs until we are in government. Office
makes Tories of us all.

FOX: Not me. God, those bells! Why do they love him so?

SHERIDAN: They can forgive the King anything for the simplicity
of his life.

FOX: Yes. The Royal Family. Fifteen children. I think his family
life is just an extension of his interest in agriculture: he can't
see a hole but he has to put a seed in it.

SHERIDAN: Well, Fox, if you hate the father, you ought to hate
the son.

FOX: How can I? The Prince hates his father more than I do.

BURKE: But I'm sure it's just this king you hate.

FOX: No it isn't. It's the institution. The breed. I loathe all kings.
And if a few ramshackle colonists in America can send him
packing, why can't we?

BURKE: No, no. Limit his powers, yes, but a republic, God
forbid. No, we must persevere, opposing every measure Pitt
brings forward.

(MRS ARMISTEAD, *Fox's mistress, now appears to collect* FOX.)

MRS ARMISTEAD: Mr Fox.

FOX: (*Apologetically*) Actually, Mrs Armistead and I were thinking of a continental holiday.

BURKE: A holiday? From the struggle? No, Fox. Not now. Your place is here.

FOX: Why? All I do is play cards with the Prince.

MRS ARMISTEAD: Mr Fox has promised there's going to be no more cards.

FOX: There's going to be *less* cards, Mrs Armistead.

SHERIDAN: And when are you coming back?

(FOX *looks sheepish.*)

FOX: Soon. A year.

BURKE: A *year!*

SHERIDAN: Is it money?

FOX: No.

MRS ARMISTEAD: Is it, Mr Fox?

FOX: If I had been in government there is so much I could have done.

SHERIDAN: We helped to found America.

FOX: Pitt was on our side then. Now he has stitched himself into the flag and passed himself off as the spirit of the nation and the Tories as the collective virtue of England. Well, it's over. I am now going to turn my back on this piss-stained ammoniacal little country and that rat-run the House of Commons . . .

MRS ARMISTEAD: Yes, dear.

FOX: . . . We're going to Lausanne to visit Gibbon . . .

SHERIDAN: Very fat now, they say.

FOX: . . . Weimar to see Goethe. We shall look at pictures.

MRS ARMISTEAD: Go to the play.

FOX: Read.

MRS ARMISTEAD: But not newspapers.

FOX: Write.

MRS ARMISTEAD: But not pamphlets.

FOX: And with Mrs Armistead's help I shall be cured of politics and turn my back once and for all on this rancid little island and its anal fistula of a King. Let Pitt and his cronies ply

5

their tireless tongues up that ex-Silesian sphincter, I do not care.

(*They go.*)

BURKE: But he does. He does. Still, it's a sad sight, Sheridan. A man giving up politics.

SHERIDAN: If you believe him.

BURKE: Could you give it up?

SHERIDAN: As distinct from the theatre, you mean? I don't know. There's the drama, of course. The temperament. And the acting, I suppose.

BURKE: What would you miss about politics?

SHERIDAN: I'm talking about politics.

(*They are going.*)

BURKE: Incidentally, who is Mr Armistead?

SHERIDAN: Oh, I think he's a figure of speech.

WINDSOR

There is a burst of Handel as PITT *enters with a despatch box. He is followed by the* PAGES, *one with a portable desk, another with an inkstand.*

PAGES: The King, the King.

(*When the* KING *appears* PITT *bows deeply* (*as does everyone whenever the* KING *enters; the Court is of stifling formality*). PITT *then takes documents from the despatch box, which the* KING *reads and signs at the portable desk, all of which is covered by music.*

Meanwhile a handsome and disdainful equerry, CAPTAIN FITZROY, *instructs a new equerry,* GREVILLE, *in his duties.*)

FITZROY: His Majesty is very fond of Handel, Greville, are you?

GREVILLE: I am not familiar with his music, Captain Fitzroy.

FITZROY: You will be. His Majesty does nothing by halves. If he is fond of a thing, be it Handel or mutton and potatoes, by God he will have it whenever occasion permits. His mode of life is simple and he is harnessed to routine. You will appreciate from what I have been saying that to be equerry to His Majesty is not the liveliest of situations.

GREVILLE: I am anxious only to be of service.

FITZROY: Quite so.

KING: Married yet, Mr Pitt, what, what?

PITT: No, sir.

KING: Got your eye on anybody then, hey?

PITT: No, sir.

KING: More to the point – anybody got their eye on you, hey hey?

PITT: Not to my knowledge, sir.

KING: A man should marry. Yes, yes. Best thing I ever did. Queen's a treasure. Not a beauty, not a beauty, but the better for it. Character what counts, eh, what, what?

PITT: Nearly done, sir.

KING: And children, you see. Children. Great comfort. Except they die, of course. Octavius, we lost. Lovely little fellow. Yes, yes.

(*He looks at one of the warrants he is signing.*)

This chap we're putting in as professor at Oxford, was his father Canon of Westminster?

PITT: I've no idea, sir.

KING: Yes, yes. Phillips, yes. That's the father. This is the son. And the daughter married the organist of Norwich Cathedral. Sharpe. Whose son is the painter. Yes. And the other son is a master at Eton. And he married somebody . . .

PITT: Your Majesty's knowledge of even the lowliest of your appointments never ceases to astonish me.

KING: What's happened to Fox?

PITT: He's abroad at the present, sir.

KING: We must hope he stays there. Such a dodger. And too many ideas. Not like you, Mr Pitt. You don't have ideas. Well, you have one big idea: balancing the books. And a very good idea to have, what, what? The best. And one with which I absolutely agree, as I agree with you, Mr Pitt, on everything apart from the place we mustn't mention.

(*He gives* PITT *a sidelong look.* PITT *says nothing.*)

We didn't see eye to eye over that, but we agreed to draw a veil over it. And I'm only mentioning it now just to show that I haven't mentioned it. You know where I mean, what?

PITT: Yes, sir.

7

KING: The colonies.

PITT: They're now called the United States, sir.

KING: Are they? Goodness me! Well, I haven't mentioned them. I prefer not to, whatever they're called. The United States. (*There is a momentary hesitation on the words 'United States', as if the* KING *finds them difficult to articulate. Noted by the* PAGES *and the* EQUERRIES *and also by* PITT, *it quickly passes.*) When I think about them . . . and I'm not thinking about them in particular . . . but when people in Parliament oppose, go against my wishes, I still find it very vexing. Try as I can, it seems to me disloyalty.

PITT: Your Majesty should not take it so personally.

KING: Not take it personally? But I'm King. This is my government. How else am I supposed to take it but personally?

PITT: The Whigs believe it is their duty to oppose you, sir.

KING: Duty? Duty? What sort of duty is that?

PITT: The House is very quiet at the moment, sir.

KING: Well, you must try and keep it that way, what, what? And we'll get a lot more done. Good night, Mr Pitt.

PITT: Good night, Your Majesty.
(*The* KING *is going. He stops.*)

KING: The Vicar of Lichfield.

PITT: Sir?

KING: Vicar of Lichfield. That's whom the daughter of the organist of Norwich Cathedral married. Hmm. Good. Good.
(*The* KING *leaves, followed by* PITT, *and* FITZROY *resumes his instruction. A* MAID *with a warming pan crosses the stage.*)

FITZOY: Having risen punctually at six, His Majesty retires to bed punctually at eleven, though, since kings like to be ruled by clocks, it is all punctual. It is a regular succession of occupations chequered occasionally by the varieties of the moment. Some would and do call it dull . . .

PAGES: Sharp! Sharp! The King! The King!
(*The* KING *comes on, now in his dressing-gown but still reading and signing papers.*)

FITZROY: But monarchs like their days populous and determined. To be idle or alone are pools in which they might glimpse themselves. To lead them past such pools and mitigate their solitude is the whole duty of courtiers.

(*The* MAID *with the warming pan returns and the* KING *stops her.*)

KING: All done, hey? Bed warm, is it? What?

MAID: Sir.

KING: Got enough coal in, have you? (*He opens the warming pan and looks inside, using his nightshirt to hold the hot handle.*) Know where this coal comes from, what?

MAID: The cellar, sir.

KING: (*Laughing*) No, no, Kent. That's good Kent coal, what. Off you go.

FITZROY: His Majesty is nothing if not inquisitive, and interests himself in every department of the nation's endeavours. His curiosity is benevolent, undirected. And infinite.

(*And from* FITZROY'*s tone, infinitely wearing.*)

All in all, he is a most cultivated fellow.

(*There now appears the statuesque figure of the Queen's Mistress of the Robes,* LADY PEMBROKE, *carrying a candlestick. Tall, distinguished (and around fifty), she is an impressive sight.*)

KING: Ready?

LADY PEMBROKE: Sir.

KING: You the new equerry, are you, what?

GREVILLE: Your Majesty.

KING: Greville, Good, good. Well that's Lady Pembroke. Handsome woman, what? Daughter of the Duke of Marlborough. Stuff of generals. Blood of Blenheim. Husband an utter rascal. Eloped in a packet-boat. Yes.

(*All leave (backwards as ever) as* LADY PEMBROKE *conducts the* KING *into the presence of the* QUEEN, *before withdrawing herself. The* QUEEN *is in bed, knitting.*)

KING: Good evening, Mrs King.

QUEEN: Good evening, Mr King.

KING: When we get this far I call it dandy, hey?

QUEEN: Indeed, Mr King.

KING: Is it hot?

QUEEN: No, sir.

KING: I am hot. Feel my belly.

9

QUEEN: It rumbles, sir.

KING: I ate a pear at supper.

QUEEN: Two pears, sir. It is as tight as a drum.

KING: Saving your presence I will try a fart.

(*The* QUEEN *indicates he should get out of bed first. Grumbling he does so, but it is no use.*)

QUEEN: No?

(*He shakes his head and gets back in again.*)

Lady Townshend came to see me this evening.

KING: Yes?

QUEEN: Wanted to know if she could sit during the drawing room.

KING: Sit – what on earth for?

QUEEN: She is about to give birth.

KING: So? You gave birth fifteen times.

QUEEN: Yes, but I do sit.

KING: Hmm, well, nothing wrong with standing. It's only two hours. What did you say?

QUEEN: Told her she should stand.

KING: Quite right. If everybody who is having a child starts sitting the next thing it'll be everybody with gout, and before long the place'll look like a Turkish harem, what, what. Cold fish, Pitt. Never smiles. Works though, oh yes. Never stops. Drinks, they say. But then they all drink. His father went mad. Doesn't show any sign of that. Pain in my belly now. Oh, Charlotte!

QUEEN: Oh, George!

(*He begins to cry out.*)

KING: Oh, oh!

(*A curtain is quickly drawn across the scene as* GREVILLE *enters with* SIR GEORGE BAKER, *the King's first physician.*)

BAKER: When did this bilious attack come on?

GREVILLE: In the early hours of the morning.

BAKER: Was His Majesty in pain?

GREVILLE: Crying out with it.

BAKER: I sent over some senna. Was that given to him?

GREVILLE: Yes. The pain got worse.

BAKER: Whereabouts was the pain?

GREVILLE: Would it not be better to ask His Majesty that?

BAKER: How long have you been in waiting? I cannot address His Majesty until he addresses me. I cannot enquire after His Majesty's symptoms until he chooses to inform me of them.

GREVILLE: Sir George. Whatever his situation His Majesty is but a man . . .

BAKER: You're the King's equerry with radical notions like that? Good God. With any patient I undertake a physical examination only as a last resort; it is an intolerable intrusion on a gentleman's privacy. With His Majesty it is unthinkable. However, it's probably only a fever – a tax our constitutions must pay for this dreadful climate.
(*Shouts of* 'The King! The King! Sharp! Sharp!' *The* KING *comes in.*)

GREVILLE: Here is your physician, sir.

KING: Yes, Baker. A ninny, what, what. Tell him I am much better. I had a pretty smart bilious attack, very smart indeed, but it has passed.

BAKER: Sir. Would it be possible to take His Majesty's pulse?

GREVILLE: Would it be . . .

KING: Yes, yes. Here. Do it. Do it, sir, do it. Do not faff, sir. And firm, sir. Hold it, do not fondle it. This is the way you take a pulse, what? One two three four five six seven eight, what, what. Go on, go on.

BAKER: I've lost count, sir.

KING: Now. Were you responsible for the senna, Baker?

BAKER: I prescribed it for Your Majesty, yes, sir.

KING: Then you are a fool, Baker, what, what?

BAKER: It's just a mild purgative, sir.

KING: Mild, sir, mild? Fourteen motions and you call it mild. I could have manured the whole parish. Where does it originate, this senna, what, what?

BAKER: The tropics – Africa, America, sir.

KING: America, ah! Well, I want no more of it. If two glasses of it can bring the King low, it could be the end of all government.

BAKER: Two glasses! Your Majesty was only supposed to take three spoonfuls.

KING: When did three spoonfuls of anything do anybody any good? Measure the medicine to the man, Baker. How is my pulse?

BAKER: It's very fast, sir.

KING: Good, good.

BAKER: Your Majesty would probably feel better after a warm bath. A warm bath has a settling effect on the spirits.

KING: You have one, then. Your spirits are more agitated than mine.

(*The* QUEEN *has come in with* LADY PEMBROKE.)

FORTNUM: Her Majesty the Queen, Your Majesty.

QUEEN: Well, Sir George, how is His Majesty?

BAKER: His pulse is far too fast, Your Majesty.

KING: Rubbish.

QUEEN: Your Majesty works too hard. Perhaps we should have a holiday. Take the waters.

KING: The waters, eh? Perhaps we should. Where do people go nowadays, Elizabeth, eh?

LADY PEMBROKE: Bath, sir. Cheltenham.

KING: Cheltenham, eh?

QUEEN: The son goes to Cheltenham.

KING: Well, so shall we. Progress through Gloucestershire. Loyal addresses, what? Keys of the city. People on every hand. Hooray, hooray! God save the King, what, what?

QUEEN: Do not excite yourself, sir.

KING: Take Elizabeth, of course. You know Cheltenham I suppose, what?

LADY PEMBROKE: Yes, sir.

KING: What do you think of it?

LADY PEMBROKE: It is much resorted to by people of fashion, sir.

KING: People of fashion, Mrs King. Do you hear that? Take a little house. No levées or drawing rooms, no talking to people we don't wish to talk to. Live like an ordinary couple. Mr and Mrs King. People of fashion!

There is a flourish and music and the curtain is drawn to reveal
FITZROY, GREVILLE *and* BAKER *being interviewed by* THURLOW,
DUNDAS, *a refined Scot, and* PITT, *who as ever holds himself aloof
from the proceedings.*

THURLOW: Gossip, gossip, gossip. Still, we'd better hear the rest
of it.

FITZROY: Having left Cheltenham they lodged at Worcester, in
the palace of Bishop Hurd, where the King rose before
dawn, went round to the Dean's lodgings, and by persistent
battering on the door roused the Dean and commanded him
to show him the cathedral.

THURLOW: Well?

BAKER: Lord Chancellor, it was still dark.

PITT: His Majesty sounds in his customary rude health.

BAKER: But the early rising? The visit to the Dean?

DUNDAS: What time would you have him rise? Five? Six? Is there
an hour consistent with rationality?

THURLOW: Dammit, man, Mr Fox is seldom in bed by five. You
doctors would have us all in Bedlam.

GREVILLE: It is true His Majesty is an early riser.

FITZROY: He walks about unattended by the court.

THURLOW: At five in the morning? You should be grateful!

BAKER: When he takes the waters, whereas others take a glass he
dashes back several bumpers.

PITT: Have we come to the end of this catalogue of regal
nonconformities? Because I have heard nothing to suggest
His Majesty's behaviour is in any way unusual. It was after
all a holiday. Now that he is back at Windsor he will
doubtless settle down.

FITZROY: He also harps on America. The colonies.
(*At this* PITT *turns and looks, and there is a slight pause.* PITT
nods to DUNDAS.)

DUNDAS: That will be all. But Captain Fitzroy, for the strongest
reasons, both foreign and domestic, a degree of discretion.

THURLOW: Yes. Goddamit, man. Keep your mouth shut. It's all
tittle-tattle.

13

(FITZROY *and* GREVILLE *go.*)

BAKER: The colic's not tittle-tattle. The sweats are not tittle-tattle, nor the pains in the legs. Though I have not been well myself lately.

THURLOW: What do you think it is?

BAKER: I may have caught a chill.

THURLOW: Not you, man. His Majesty.

BAKER: It may be that he has caught rheumatism in his legs and it has flown to his stomach. Or gout, of course.

DUNDAS: He scarcely drinks.

BAKER: *Flying* gout.

THURLOW: I have been assured that the sovereign remedy for gout is to cut the toenails in hot water.

BAKER: It may be.

THURLOW: God's teeth. You're President of the Royal College of Physicians. You ought to know.

BAKER: I did however venture to take his pulse. It has become languid.

(*He absentmindedly takes* THURLOW'*s.*)

THURLOW: Languid? What does that mean?

BAKER: Well, yours you see is hard and wiry.

THURLOW: And?

BAKER: There are physicians who believe that we each have our fixed allotment of heartbeats, and that a hard pulse such as this one uses up that deposit of heartbeats quicker than a languid one.

THURLOW: Good God, really? Then there is an economy here too. (*He feels his pulse.*) How do I slow it down?

DUNDAS: You will keep us informed?

BAKER: I am at Windsor every day.

(*Leaving,* BAKER *bows to* PITT, *who ignores him.*)

DUNDAS: At thirty guineas a time I'm not surprised.

THURLOW: Hard and wiry. What's yours like?

PITT: I can't believe he's that ill. Baker makes out he is so that when in due course he recovers, Baker gets the credit. I've done the same myself. Before we came in I said the nation was sick, deliberately predicted national bankruptcy, so that when the economy recovered, prosperity was put

14

down to me. No, he is not ill.

THURLOW: Well, I don't like it. Though there was a mysterious illness once before, in your father's time. Government was at a standstill.

DUNDAS: It was of no consequence.

THURLOW: It was of no consequence because he recovered.

PITT: It was of no consequence because the Prince of Wales was then a child of three. It was of no consequence because Mr Fox and his friends were not perched in the rafters waiting to come in. We consider ourselves blessed in our constitution. We tell ourselves our parliament is the envy of the world. But we live in the health and well-being of the Sovereign as much as any vizier does the Sultan.

THURLOW: And the Sultan orders it better. He has his son and heir strangled.

CARLTON HOUSE

The PRINCE OF WALES, *the* DUKE OF YORK, SHERIDAN, BURKE *and the Prince's physician,* DR RICHARD WARREN, *are listening to* FITZROY, *who is telling his tale here too and plainly much more at ease than in the previous scene, even lounging in a chair.*

FITZROY: His Majesty then downed three bumpers of the spa water. The effect on his system I will not venture to describe.

PRINCE OF WALES: We are grateful for your forbearance, Captain Fitzroy. And what does Mr Pitt say to all this?

FITZROY: Mr Pitt professes not to find in the reports any departure from His Majesty's customary behaviour.

DUKE OF YORK: What, what.

PRINCE OF WALES: Hey, hey.

BOTH: Farmer George, pigs, what. (*Snort, snort.*)

PRINCE OF WALES: Well, Warren, what do you make of it?

WARREN: Diagnosis is difficult unless I see His Majesty.

PRINCE OF WALES: You're not likely to. The King is more likely to go to my tailor than my doctor.

WARREN: But I take the gravest view of his symptoms.

DUKE OF YORK: (*Reading the report*) His Majesty's discourse is
    sporadic. What's that?
SHERIDAN: Fits and starts, sir.
DUKE OF YORK: Usual thing, you mean.
FITZROY: He hardly sleeps.
SHERIDAN: And is often in excruciating pain.
PRINCE OF WALES: Oh. Poor pa. There's no danger . . . is there?
    (WARREN *says nothing.*)
    Dear me. Death, Fred.
DUKE OF YORK: Gosh.
WARREN: Or if not death a state of mind so tenuous as to make
    His Majesty unfit to govern.
PRINCE OF WALES: Mad, Fred.
DUKE OF YORK: Oh dear.
SHERIDAN: Pitt will have to recall Parliament and if His Majesty
    is ill your Royal Highness must in due course be declared
    Regent.
PRINCE OF WALES: Regent?
SHERIDAN: King in all but name.
PRINCE OF WALES: Regent. With all the powers?
SHERIDAN: Yes.
BURKE: It's quite interesting constitutionally. One would have to go
    back to the fifteenth century for a situation at all similar . . .
PRINCE OF WALES: (*Ignoring* BURKE) And all the funds?
SHERIDAN: Oh yes.
PRINCE OF WALES: Where's Fox? We'd better send for him.
SHERIDAN: Bologna. Lying on the conscientious bosom of Mrs
    Armistead.
DUKE OF YORK: Bet that's sporadic. Fits and starts there, what.
PRINCE OF WALES: Fred, please. Pa is ill.
DUKE OF YORK: Sorry, Prin.
SHERIDAN: It would be best, sir, if in this matter of His Majesty's
    health we should be seen to disclaim any party advantage.
PRINCE OF WALES: Quite agree. Quite agree. Why exactly?
SHERIDAN: A month or so ago Pitt looked set for another ten
    years. Now we have a chance to turn him out because the
    King is ill, but we must not seem over-eager, lest we be
    thought unpatriotic or self-seeking.

16

PRINCE OF WALES: A son who must . . . reluctantly . . . shoulder the responsibilities of a sick – who knows, possibly a dying father – that is hardly self-seeking.

SHERIDAN: But it must be reluctantly.

PRINCE OF WALES: Of course. A necessary duty; a task unshirked. No joy in it. No joy in it at all. Windsor would have to be entirely altered, of course. It's impossible as it is.

DUKE OF YORK: And meanwhile mum's the word, what?

PRINCE OF WALES: Mum is not the word. The King is indisposed. He has a special place in the hearts of his people. They must be told and told forthwith.

SHERIDAN: In that case, sir, your brother is right, and you would do better to proclaim it a secret.

DUKE OF YORK: Hey, hey.

PRINCE OF WALES: Why?

SHERIDAN: Because if it is a secret, by the common course of things it must reach the Duchess of Devonshire's ears by dusk, and then the whole of London will know by morning.

WINDSOR

The curtains have been drawn across the full width of the stage and the KING *in his nightshirt begins to pull them back.*

KING: Where are you, sirs? Fortnum! Papandiek! What is this? The King is unattended. Up with you. Papandiek.
(PAPANDIEK *rushes on in his nightshirt (a shorter version than the King's). He is the kindest of the pages and the one with a genuine concern for his master.*)

PAPANDIEK: What's the matter, sir?
(FORTNUM *hurries in, still dressing.*)

KING: The matter is, sir, that it is morning. That is the matter. Morning is the matter. Not being attended to is the matter. And don't mutter. Or mutter will be the matter.

PAPANDIEK: What time is it, sir?

KING: What is that to you? The King is up. You attend on the King, not on the clock. When the King is awake, you are awake. It is four o'clock. Six hours' sleep is enough for a man,

17

seven for a woman, and eight for a fool.

FORTNUM: Then we've only had three. We didn't go to bed till one.

KING: Is that insolence, sir?

FORTNUM: No, sir. Arithmetic.

(*The* KING *tries to strike him.*)

KING: What's your name?

FORTNUM: Fortnum, sir.

KING: Fetch me my breeches.

(*Enter* BRAUN.)

BRAUN: What's all this damned noise? Has the old boy rung?

KING: Yes, he has rung. He has been ringing for half-an-hour. Lazy
hound. Stir yourself, boy. Lazy, lazy, lazy. Find my breeches.

PAPANDIEK: I have them, sir.

KING: What is your name, sir?

PAPANDIEK: You know my name, sir.

KING: Don't tell me what I know and don't know. What is it?

PAPANDIEK: Papandiek, sir. Arthur, sir.

KING: (*Peering at him*) Is it Arthur? And you?

FORTNUM: Fortnum, sir.

KING: Well, hold me, boys, hold me. Or I shall fall.

PAPANDIEK: It's all this hurry and flurry, sir. If Your Majesty
would just lift your leg.

KING: I am the King. You lift my leg. Oh . . . oh . . . (*He is falling
over.*)

PAPANDIEK: I have you, sir.

KING: Why do you shiver? I am not cold. I am warm. I am
burning. No, I am not burning. It is my body that is
burning. And I am locked inside it, Arthur. Where's that
other rascal Braun? He's not gone back to bed?

BRAUN: I'm here, sir.

KING: Well, give me my shirt then. What shirt is this?

PAPANDIEK: Your shirt, sir.

KING: No. It's rough. Feel. It's like calico. Sailcloth. It's a
hairshirt.

BRAUN: It's linen, sir, and laundered yesterday.

KING: How long have you been in my service?

BRAUN: Your Majesty knows.

KING: How should I know, sir, if I ask. How long?

18

BRAUN: Three years, sir. And before that I was in the service of
the Prince of Wales. Those were the days. None of this four
o'clock in the morning game. And a drink now and again.

KING: Do not talk of the Prince, sir. Who has put you up to
talking of the Prince? Fortnum, have you sons?

FORTNUM: I am not married, sir.

KING: That will not save you. Fetch me another.

BRAUN: Another what, sir?

KING: Another shirt, sir. A softer shirt. You've brought this up to
scratch. Go, go.
(PAPANDIEK *and* FORTNUM *are putting on his stockings.*)
Do not snatch and pull, sir.

FORTNUM: I am not snatching and pulling, sir.

KING: I am the King. You are pulling, sir.

FORTNUM: Yes, sir.

KING: Stop, you clumsy oaf. Arthur, you do it.
(BRAUN *returns with another shirt.*)

PAPANDIEK: Your Majesty's legs are tender.

KING: These are not my proper stockings.

PAPANDIEK: Sir?

KING: They itch, too. I burn all inward. My limbs are laced with
fire. But I will not give in to it. Have you said your prayers
this morning?

BRAUN: I started, sir, but I was interrupted.

KING: Say after me – Our Father, which art in heaven . . .
(*As the* KING *leads the pages in the Lord's Prayer, the* QUEEN
and LADY PEMBROKE, *still in their nightclothes, come anxiously
down the stairs accompanied by* GREVILLE, *who is also half
dressed, and* BAKER.
The KING *suddenly catches sight of* LADY PEMBROKE.)
Oh God, my blood is full of cramps, lobsters crack my
bones, there are stones in my belly. Oh, Elizabeth!
(*He embraces* LADY PEMBROKE *and kisses her full on the lips.*)

QUEEN: Sir, we are in company.

KING: Mind your own business.

LADY PEMBROKE: You must rest, sir.

KING: No. I am the King. I cannot rest. I must rule. Half the day
gone already. There is much to do, there is government . . .

PAPANDIEK: Government hasn't begun yet, sir. Government is in bed.

BRAUN: Government is lucky.

(*The* KING *rushes off.*

GREVILLE *hurries after him, gathering up the pages.*)

GREVILLE: Follow, follow.

QUEEN: Well, Baker, what is to be done?

BAKER: His Majesty must be bled. If only he will keep still. Forgive me – (*Wanting to go after the King.*)

QUEEN: Yes, yes. Go! Mr Pitt must be informed.

(*The* QUEEN *and* LADY PEMBROKE *are left alone. There is an awkward silence.*)

Elizabeth.

LADY PEMBROKE: Ma'am.

QUEEN: His Majesty is not himself.

LADY PEMBROKE: No, ma'am.

QUEEN: Something has got into him. He has been a faithful husband. Though he does not lack opportunity. What was your husband like – Lord Pembroke?

LADY PEMBROKE: A fiend, ma'am.

QUEEN: In what way?

LADY PEMBROKE: In the usual way, ma'am.

QUEEN: Elizabeth, if the King should pay you undue attention, it means nothing. You must try and ignore it.

LADY PEMBROKE: Yes, ma'am.

(*Pause.*)

Ma'am.

QUEEN: (*Surprised to be spoken to*) Yes?

LADY PEMBROKE: So must Your Majesty.

(*The* QUEEN *looks less certain about this but they go as* FORTNUM, *coming on with a glass chamber pot, runs into* BRAUN.)

FORTNUM: Look.

BRAUN: What?

FORTNUM: It's blue.

(*He holds the pot up to the light and we see that the piss is dark blue. There is a hint of music which, though not quite the Lilac Fairy, should focus the attention.*)

BRAUN: I'd call it purple. You and me, we piss plain. Kings piss purple.
(FITZROY *enters*.)
FITZROY: What are you dawdling here for? The King is unattended.
FORTNUM: It's this, sir.
FITZROY: What?
FORTNUM: The King's water, sir. It's blue, sir.
BRAUN: Purple.
FORTNUM: It's been this colour since this business began.
FITZROY: What business? Don't be insolent.
FORTNUM: We thought it might be important.
FITZROY: What is important is not to dangle about. Where is His Majesty? Unattended, and half undressed. That's what's important. Give me that.
(*He takes the chamber-pot. The pages go off as* BAKER *enters, an apron on, ready to bleed the King.*)
Sir George . . . I . . . This is the King's water.
BAKER: I'm not interested in his water. I'm about to bleed him.
FITZROY: It's blue.
BAKER: So?
FITZROY: It has been blue since His Majesty has been ill.
BAKER: Oh God, another doctor. Medicine is a science. It consists of observation. Whether a man's water is blue or not is neither here nor there.
(*He goes, leaving the chamber-pot with* FITZROY *who, not knowing what to do with it, eventually carries it off at arm's length.*)
FITZROY: Well, there's one blessing. At least he's stopped all the what-whatting.

WINDSOR

DUNDAS: The Prince hasn't wasted any time. He's banking on Parliament being recalled, so poor Fox has had to say farewell to Mrs Armistead and is now pelting back.
(PITT *says nothing*.)

It's a pity Sir has no Mrs Armistead. Half the trouble, to my mind. Cork too tight in the bottle. What is wanting with HM is a little quiet dissipation. A King and no mistress. Or anyone in a lofty situation. It's unheard of.

PITT: It has been known.

(*It is* PITT's *own situation, after all.*)

DUNDAS: I'm sorry. But I'm right, am I not? The man has to break out. I would suffocate here.

PITT: Fifteen children seem to me to indicate a degree of conscientiousness in that regard.

DUNDAS: I'm talking of pleasure, not duty.

PITT: They are a devoted couple.

DUNDAS: The bloom has at any rate gone off the Queen's ugliness. Since she fell from her carriage and broke her nose she's quite handsome.

PITT: I do not think the King appreciates that he cannot afford to be ill. I shall point out to him that if he is ill for any length of time the Government will fall. That is the best medicine.

(*Enter* THURLOW *in a flurry.*)

THURLOW: I thought I was late. Then he really would be mad.

(PITT *looks but says nothing.*)

I've been in the City. The stocks are down again and they expect a run on the Bank. Some damn fool must have talked.

PITT: Everybody talks.

THURLOW: Not tittle-tattle. Somebody who might be expected to know. Though there is tittle-tattle, of course. I was told that it all started because His Majesty was annoyed with the Duke of York for trying to introduce Turkish instruments into the band of the Guards.

DUNDAS: Yes, that would send anybody mad.

PITT: I would be obliged if you did not use that word.

DUNDAS: What word?

PITT: Mad. He is no madder than the generality.

(FITZROY *comes in, and through the door we hear a babble of excited German.*)

FITZROY: His Majesty sends his compliments and will receive you shortly.

22

THURLOW: Any change?

(FITZROY *disdains even to answer the question.*)

PITT: Captain Fitzroy. I sent a box of the most urgent papers requiring His Majesty's signature. Has he dealt with them?

FITZROY: No, sir.

(*He goes back in to the King's room.*)

PITT: Some of them are a month old. Government is at a halt.

THURLOW: You have been spoiled. A king never behind with his boxes. That's half the trouble. Too conscientious.

PITT: These are appointments, pensions, jobs. Votes. An ailing King means an ailing Government.

THURLOW: So there's a lull in government. The country will be grateful. There's too much damned Government.

(*The door opens again and* BAKER *backs through it.*)

BAKER: I have every hope of a cure, Your Majesty.

KING: (*Off*) Cure, you cretin? You couldn't cure a gammon ham.

BAKER: No, Your Majesty.

KING: (*Off*) Push off, you fat turd.

BAKER: Yes, Your Majesty. No, Your Majesty.

(*The door closes.*)

Oh, Lord Chancellor, I should not have to put up with this.

THURLOW: Why? You're being paid.

DUNDAS: How is the King?

BAKER: The same. Worse. He varies. His tongue runs away with him. Thoughts that a well man keeps under he just babbles forth.

PITT: Is he fit to be seen?

BAKER: By whom?

PITT: In public. He has to be seen or he will be thought dying and the stocks fall further.

BAKER: Have they fallen again? Oh dear. My broker was expecting a run on the bank.

THURLOW: Your broker, Baker?

BAKER: Yes.

THURLOW: And what were you doing with your broker, Baker?

BAKER: Well, what does one do with one's broker? One has affairs.

THURLOW: Not selling stock?

BAKER: I may have sold a little.

THURLOW: So it was you, sir.

BAKER: Me, sir? No, sir! What, sir?

THURLOW: Fool! Drivelling idiot!

BAKER: Sir, I am President of the Royal College of Physicians.

THURLOW: Yes, and Secretary of the Royal Institute of Blabbers.
You have started a run on the Bank, sir.

BAKER: Me, sir? No, sir!

THURLOW: The King's doctor sells his stock, ergo the King is not
expected to recover.

BAKER: I am a poor man. I have my family to think of.

(PITT *takes little notice of all this, but as the* KING *is announced
gathers up his papers and stands up.*)

PAGES: Sharp, sharp. The King. The King.

BAKER: Oh, no more. No more.

(*He bolts from the room as* FITZROY *opens the door. The* PAGES
*come in with the desk, the inkstand, etc., but it is some moments
before the* KING *appears, legs bandaged and moving very slowly.
He peers about him.*)

KING: Mr Pitt? Mr Pitt? You see us suddenly an old man.

GREVILLE: Will Your Majesty not sit down?

(FITZROY *heaves a sigh of disapproval.*)

KING: The King never sits when seeing his ministers. Sits, no.
Shits though, yes. They say I soiled my small clothes this
morning. It is not true. Or it may be true. My flesh is on fire.
I must quench it whatever way comes to hand. Dundas, yes?
(*Peers.*)

DUNDAS: Your Majesty.

KING: The Scots one. Thurlow?

THURLOW: Your Majesty.

KING: Father was Rector of Ashfield. Brother's Bishop of
Durham. Shaggy fellow. Yes. Why do you look at me? Do
not look at me. I am the King. Speak, speak.

PITT: Perhaps I can lay before Your Majesty some of the more
urgent papers awaiting Your Majesty's signature.

(*The* KING *motions for them.*)

KING: Mr Pitt, I do not see so well. There is no mist here?

PITT: No, sir.

24

KING: Oh, my aching brain. What is this? (*Looking at the paper*) America, is it?

PITT: No, sir. It is a warrant for the most urgent expenditure. I beg Your Majesty to sign it.

KING: America is not to be spoken of, is that it?

PITT: For your own peace of mind, sir. But it is not America. It is a warrant for –

KING: Peace of mind! I have no peace of mind. I have had no peace of mind since we lost America. Forests, old as the world itself, meadows, plains, strange delicate flowers, immense solitudes. And all nature new to art. All ours. Mine. Gone. A paradise lost. The trumpet of sedition has sounded. We have lost America. Soon we shall lose India, the Indies, Ireland even, our feathers plucked one by one, this island reduced to itself alone, a great state mouldered into rottenness and decay. And they will lay it at my door. What is this I am reading? It *is* America. The words fly ahead of me. I cannot catch them in the mist.

PITT: If Your Majesty would trust me, it would assist your ministers immeasurably if Your Majesty would just sign the warrants. It is most urgent, I assure you.

KING: But I have to read them. I do not sign anything I do not read. I might be signing my own deposition. Is that why you are gathered?

THURLOW: No, sir. We are your loyal servants, sir. In your present frame of mind . . .

KING: What do you know of my mind? Or its frame? Something is shaking the frame; shaking the mind out of its frame. I am not going out of my mind; my mind is going out of me.
(*The* KING *begins to scratch himself or even to take off some of his clothes. He turns to leave.*)
Go, all of you.

PITT: Sir –

KING: Go, go.

PITT: I beg you, sir. Sir (*holding out the warrants for the* KING).

DUNDAS: William!
(PITT *snatches a pen from* PAPANDIEK, *seizes the writing desk from* FORTNUM *and thrusts it at the* KING. DUNDAS *tries to*

restrain him and PITT'*s loss of dignity seems even to shock the* KING.)

PITT: I beg you.

KING: Beg me what?

PITT: The warrants, sir. Your Majesty must try to be well . . . or . . . or . . . the Government will suffer.

KING: The Go . . . Go . . . Government.

(*The* KING *takes the warrant, looks at it unseeingly, hands it to* FITZROY *and goes. The* PAGES, *smoothly but with an air of disapproval, recover the pen and writing desk from* PITT *and as* FITZROY *wearily hands* PITT *the unsigned warrant they all follow the* KING *out.*)

PITT: He can see . . . so he can read. He only has to sign.

THURLOW: Being a lawyer, I have had some commerce with madness.

(PITT *looks.*)

I speak as I find. When I was a young man I was friend to one William Cowper. I saw him removed to a madhouse in St Albans. For all I know he's still there. Mind you, he was a morbid fellow. Poet.

DUNDAS: What is it like?

THURLOW: Like taking off one's braces.

DUNDAS: There is consolation in it, you mean?

THURLOW: For some. Were the King not in pain one might envy him. Saying what he likes.

(PITT *takes a swig from a hip flask, such a regular feature of his behaviour it is not noted in the stage directions.*)

PITT: I have a great disrelish for absurdity. But I will not believe it. Let us have no more talk of madness. Because I do not believe it, do you hear?

THURLOW: God give me patience! It is not what you believe. It is what Parliament believes. It is what the Prince of Wales believes. And it is what the City believes.

PITT: That is true. So long an absence will be construed. The public will think him dead. The King must be seen. It need not be too severe a junket, but he must be seen.

The curtains are drawn back and the full stage revealed, where a concert is in progress. The court is assembled, though only the KING *and* QUEEN *are seated, the* KING *beating time to the music, which is, inevitably, Handel. The* KING *is now somewhat dishevelled, one stocking rolled down, the easier to scratch his irritated leg, the sores on which are plain to be seen. He scratches at his body too, feeling himself ever more uncomfortable in it.*

KING: (*Shouting and waving his stick*) Louder! Louder! Come on, sirs, give it some stick! Forte, forte. One two three, one two three, one two three.

> (*The music gets louder. The* KING *gets up.*)

QUEEN: Hush, sir. You are talking.

KING: I know I am talking. They are playing. I am talking. Forte, fiddler, forte.

> (*The music ends. The* KING *leads the applause.*)

That was Handel. I met him once. Ordinary-looking fellow. I have his harpsichord.

> (*The assembled company have lined up to be greeted by the* KING *and, leaning on* FITZROY's *arm, he limps down the line, peering into their faces.*)

Lord Thurlow, yes. Mr Pitt. Dundas, the Scots one. Baker. Now, Baker would have me believe I have the gout. If I have the gout how could I kick the part without pain? You, sir! Kick it. Kick it, I say.

> (FITZROY *does so, with maximum disdain.*)

Is that gout? No.

> (*He goes on down the line.*)

Elbow people, knee gentlemen, bending persons, hand kissers.

> (*The* KING *has stopped in front of* DR WARREN *and the* PRINCE OF WALES *interrupts.*)

PRINCE OF WALES: Your Majesty.

KING: The Prince of Wales! What brings you to Windsor, sir?

PRINCE OF WALES: I had heard you were ill, father.

KING: Want to hump the old bird out of the nest, you great cuckoo? Get your fat hands on government, is that it?

27

PRINCE OF WALES: May I present Dr Richard Warren, Your Majesty. Dr Warren is my personal physician.

KING: He is personal physician to half of London. Well, you are not my physician, sir. No man can serve two masters.

WARREN: I am a servant of humanity, sir.

KING: Yes, and how much does humanity pay you? (How much does humanity pay him, eh, Greville?) You should tell your patient the Prince that he is too fat. Don't slouch, sir. Well, I am old and infirm. I shall not trouble you long.

PRINCE OF WALES: I wish you good health, father.

KING: Wish me, wish me? You wish me death, you plump little partridge.

PRINCE OF WALES: Hush, sir.

KING: Hush? Hush? You dare to keep the King of England from speaking his mind?
(*The* KING *turns away from the* PRINCE, *then suddenly turns back and launches himself on him; there is turmoil as* KING *and* PRINCE *fall struggling to the floor, the* KING's *hands at the* PRINCE's *neck.*)

QUEEN: Your Majesty! Sir! Sir!

WARREN: Give him air.

GREVILLE: Lie off. Lie off.
(*The* KING *is helped to his feet and pulled away by* GREVILLE *and the* PAGES.)

KING: I know your game, I know your game, he wants to see me put away.

QUEEN: No, no, sir. It is something you ate. Come away, sir.

KING: Fools, don't you see it? Then you will all be put out; first the King, then all his company.
(*He is hustled out by* GREVILLE *and* FITZROY *as the* QUEEN *returns to appeal to* PITT *and* THURLOW.)

QUEEN: It is the son, Mr Pitt. This Warren, he knows nothing. He is doctor to the son. If you are wanting to kill the father get the doctor to the son.
(*The* PRINCE *is still on the floor, being attended to by* WARREN.)
We know your game. Monster!

THURLOW: God, these foreign women.

PRINCE OF WALES: He was like a wild animal. How am I?

WARREN: Slight bruising, sir.

PRINCE OF WALES: Slight? Good God. I feel I've been hanged. And now having seen the King, what is your impression?

WARREN: Wholly demented, sir. A palsy of the brain.

PRINCE OF WALES: Do not say so, but I can believe it. Did you see his eyes? They were like blackcurrant jelly. Still, as heir to the throne I know that His Majesty bears a heavy burden. I fear the time is coming, Mr Pitt, when it is a burden we shall be forced to share.

(*Government and Opposition are now in two groups with the* PRINCE *in the middle.*)

Ah, Baker, how is the King?

BAKER: Still talking, sir, and the pulse is 104.

THURLOW: Ah. Quite wiry still.

PRINCE OF WALES: Then he is not in command of his senses?

BAKER: Not at the moment, sir.

WARREN: Nor likely to be, if I may say so, sir.

PRINCE OF WALES: In that case, as his son and heir I must make the decisions in his place.

(PITT *looks to* THURLOW *for support but he is impassive.*)

PRINCE OF WALES: Firstly, as regards His Majesty's health, Sir George will in future be partnered by my own physician, Dr Warren.

PITT: I must insist that this arrangement be subject to the approval of His Majesty's ministers.

PRINCE OF WALES: Insist? Approval? A son's concern for his sick father. What are we coming to?

THURLOW: Your Royal Highness is right. This is a family matter.

PRINCE OF WALES: I shall also consult the physicians as to whether, until his Majesty has recovered a right perspective, he should be separated from the Queen.

WARREN: Her presence undoubtedly abets his illness, sir.

PITT: I must point out, sir, that His Majesty has frequently expressed his desire never to be separated from the Queen.

SHERIDAN: But the King is not himself, Mr Pitt. He does not know his own mind.

PRINCE OF WALES: Mr Sheridan is right. And I know my mother. She puts wrong ideas into his head, and would

interfere in his treatment. No. They are better apart. We
shall see to it. Lord Chancellor. Mr Pitt.
(The PRINCE *and the* DUKE OF YORK *go*.)
BURKE: (*To* DUNDAS, *and without animosity*) There are historical
justifications for the Prince's action.
DUNDAS: We don't wish to know them.
SHERIDAN: (*Sweetly*) And of course when we form the
government we can always review the situation.
(SHERIDAN *and* BURKE *follow the* PRINCE.)
PITT: You were not much help.
THURLOW: The Prince was right. These are matters for the
family.
PITT: Family? In the House of Hanover, where the sons snap at
their father's heels and harry them into the grave? But yes,
these are domestic melodramas which any man of sensibility
would quit, were they not, projected on a larger screen, the
very groundwork of politics. The King's body is not his own.
It belongs to the nation and so it is Parliament's concern.
(*As* PITT, DUNDAS *and* THURLOW *leave, the* KING *comes
hurrying down the steps pursued by the* QUEEN, LADY
PEMBROKE, FITZROY, GREVILLE *and the pages. The* KING
*has taken off his shoes and stockings, lest they get wet, and he lifts
Lady Pembroke's dress for the same reason and drags her with
him across the floor.*)
KING: I want a bag. A bag.
QUEEN: What for?
KING: The state secrets. I must carry them with me to the grave.
London is flooded. We must take the children and flee to the
higher ground. Save Amelia, Adolphus and little Octavius.
QUEEN: Octavius is dead, sir.
KING: Who killed him? His brother? He would kill me, I know.
You too, Elizabeth. You must not drown.
QUEEN: Hush, sir. You are talking.
KING: I know I am talking. Do not tell me I talk. I follow my
words. I run after them. I am dragged at locution's tail. This
ceaseless discourse precedes me wherever I go. Telling me I
talk! I have to talk in order to keep up with my thoughts. I
thought he had taken you.

QUEEN: Who, sir?

KING: The other George. The fat one. You were not in my bed. I
thought you had deceived me with the son.

QUEEN: Sir!

KING: Still, Elizabeth comes to my bed, don't you, Elizabeth?
(*He embraces* LADY PEMBROKE *and clasps her to him. This is
too much for the* QUEEN.)

QUEEN: Leave us! Leave us. You too, Elizabeth. And you, and
you. All of you, out, all of you, out.
(*All leave, still, even though the* KING *is a distracted wreck,
bowing and backwards.*)
Now talk away.

KING: Tell me, which of us do you prefer? He sneaks into your
bed, I know. Well, do not flatter yourself, madam. He has
many women. You are just one and not even the first. Fancy,
his mother is not even the first of the son's women, think of
that. The fat hands. That young belly. Those plump thighs.
The harlot's delight.

QUEEN: Be *still*, sir. For pity's sake. Listen, George. Hear me.
(*She holds his mouth closed to stop his babble.*)
Do you think you are mad?

KING: I don't know. I don't know. Madness isn't such torment.
Madness is not half-blind. Madmen can stand. They skip!
They dance! And I talk. I talk. I hear the words so I have to
speak them. I have to empty my head of the words. *Something*
has happened. *Something* is not right. Oh, Charlotte.
(FITZROY *comes in, followed by* LADY PEMBROKE.)

QUEEN: Can we never be solitary? I told you to leave us. Go away,
sir. His Majesty and I are talking.

KING: Is it the floods? Have the waters spread?

QUEEN: Hush, sir.
(*The* KING *nods and puts his finger to his lips, as gentle and
tractable now as a few moments before he was the reverse.*)

KING: Yes. Fitzroy is right. You are right to take precautions.

FITZROY: I have been instructed by His Royal Highness to move
Your Majesty's lodgings, ma'am . . .

QUEEN: Why? Where?

FITZROY: It is to assist His Majesty's recovery, ma'am.

31

QUEEN: But I am the Queen.

FITZROY: Your Majesty is not to have access to the King's presence, ma'am.

QUEEN: Not have access . . . You mean I am not permitted to see the King.

KING: What is this not permitted? Not permitted?

QUEEN: No, no.

FITZROY: The contents of your apartments have already been transferred, ma'am.

(*He leads the* KING *out.*)

QUEEN: No, George. Stop. What are you doing? Where are you taking the King? No. Stop. George. Your Majesty. George!

KING: (*Escorted out by* FITZROY) The water is rising. We must all move. Find the children. Gather them together. The Queen must come too. She will drown if she remains.

FITZROY: She will come, sir. She is coming.

(*As the* KING *goes out of one door the* PRINCE OF WALES *and* WARREN *come in through the other.*)

PRINCE OF WALES: Madam.

QUEEN: Booby! Tyrant! Toad! Clown!

PRINCE OF WALES: Assaulted by both one's parents in the same evening! What is family life coming to? Control yourself, madam.

QUEEN: My apartments have been invaded, my lodgings transferred, my belongings conveyed to a distant location, and now I am told I can no longer see my husband. This is your father, sir. *Ruhe. Ruhe.*

PRINCE OF WALES: I do not know what is this '*ruhe*', madam.

QUEEN: Peace. It is peace.

PRINCE OF WALES: No, madam. While you are together there will be no peace.

QUEEN: On what authority is this done?

PRINCE OF WALES: On medical authority, ma'am, on the authority of a son, ma'am, who cares for his sick father.

QUEEN: I am his wife. Do I not care for him too?

PRINCE OF WALES: Perhaps, madam. But in his current frame of mind His Majesty does not seem to care for you. His affections do not that way tend.

(*He looks at* LADY PEMBROKE, *and he and* WARREN *go*.)

QUEEN: Fiend! Monster!

LADY PEMBROKE: Come, madam. I will show you where they have lodged us.

WESTMINSTER

The curtain is pulled back to reveal DRS BAKER, WARREN *and* SIR LUCAS PEPYS. THURLOW *comes in*.

THURLOW: Good morning, gentlemen. I thought it would be useful to review the situation before any further treatment was undertaken. (*Holding out his wrist to* BAKER) Try my pulse, would you, Baker? I'm here of course to represent the Government's concern and interest in this matter, but beyond that, as someone who has always had the well-being of the Prince at heart. Now, you, Baker, I know, and Dr Warren . . .

BAKER: This is Sir Lucas Pepys, whom I have taken the liberty of consulting.

THURLOW: The more the merrier. Are you familiar with His Majesty's condition?

PEPYS: I have spent a lifetime in the study of the anfractuosities of the human understanding –

THURLOW: What?

PEPYS: – the mind, sir, and its delinquencies. If it were possible I would value an early view of one of His Majesty's motions.

THURLOW: Yes? That could be arranged, couldn't it? How am I doing, Baker?

BAKER: Still pretty wiry. Ninety.

THURLOW: Hell and damnation, what's a man to do?

WARREN: Oh, the pulse varies. It doesn't signify.

THURLOW: Really? What do you think, Pepys?

PEPYS: I agree. I've always found the stool more eloquent than the pulse.

THURLOW: Indeed? Now. What the devil is the matter with the King?

WARREN: My diagnosis is that the gouty humour has settled on

33

the brain. I would begin by prescribing regular doses of James's Powders to sweat it out.

BAKER: I tried that. No effect.

WARREN: I would then suggest emetics.

BAKER: I tried that too. They made His Majesty very loose. So I then gave him some laudanum, which made him very constipated.

PEPYS: Constipation? I don't like that. Has he been bled?

BAKER: No expedient known to the most advanced medical opinion has been neglected.

THURLOW: Well, what's the outlook?

WARREN: Very grave. Unless the humour can be decoyed from the brain, His Majesty's life, and certainly his sanity, is in the utmost danger.

BAKER: I am a little more hopeful than that. Wild though His Majesty's behaviour is, his discourse is at least consistent. It is the principle on which it is based which is in error.

THURLOW: What does that mean?

BAKER: It means that though His Majesty believes London is flooded, at least he knows that it is flooded with water.

THURLOW: Well, what should it be flooded with?

BAKER: Oh . . . Turtle soup, porridge . . .

THURLOW: God. What do you suggest, Pepys?

PEPYS: An immediate purge.

THURLOW: Warren?

WARREN: He must be blistered.

BAKER: I agree, but he will never submit.

WARREN: He must be blistered on the back to draw the humours from the brain; and he must be blistered on the legs to draw the humours to the lower extremities.

BAKER: What if he refuse?

WARREN: Then he must be forced.

THURLOW: The King? Forced?

WARREN: Yes.

THURLOW: Very well – but forced gently. Pepys. If I were able to furnish you with a sample stool, would you have time to cast an eye over it for me . . .?

34

GREVILLE *accompanies the* KING, *now in his dressing-gown, into the room where the blistering is to be done; a tray of burners and hot glasses waiting, a padded stool on which he is to be bound, and* WARREN *standing ready and gloved.*

FITZROY: Your Majesty, it is the physicians' opinion that Your Majesty's health would benefit from the application of blisters to your back and legs.

KING: And it is His Majesty's opinion that the physicians' health would benefit by the application of blisters to their arse.
(*The* KING, *having seen the fearsome preparations, turns back.*)

GREVILLE: Your Majesty knows the love and esteem in which I hold Your Majesty. I beg you to submit to this treatment.
(*He bars the* KING'S *way.*)

KING: Oh, Greville, you too.

WARREN: Bind him.

FITZROY: No. This is the King.

WARREN: Bind him, I say.

FITZROY: No. *Bandage* him.
(*The* KING *struggles with* PAGES, *who take off his dressing-gown and pull him across to the blistering-stool.*)

KING: No, no. Don't touch me, damn you. I am the King. Go, tell the Queen I am assaulted. The Queen, help!

BRAUN: Let's have your robe then, sir. Off we come. That's it.

PAPANDIEK: Easy does it, sir.

FORTNUM: Come along, sir. Don't make it hard.

KING: I was the verb, the noun and the verb. Verb rules; subject: the King. I am not the subject now. Now I am the object, the King governed, the ruler ruled. I am the subordinate clause, the insubordinate George.

PAPANDIEK: Let go, Your Majesty. That's it.

BRAUN: Down we go.
(*He is pushed face down on to the stool and pinioned,* PAPANDIEK *holding his arms and* FORTNUM *his legs, while* BRAUN *looks on with evident pleasure. The* KING *begins to pray.*)

KING: Almighty God, unto whom all hearts be open, all desires

known and from whom no secrets are hid, cleanse the
thoughts of our hearts by the inspiration of thy Holy Spirit
that we may perfectly love thee and worthily magnify thy
holy name. For the sake of Jesus Christ our Lord.
(WARREN *applies cups first to the* KING's *back. The* KING
screams in agony.)
Not my skin. Not my skin. No. No.
(*Then to his legs.*) Oh Jesus help me. For pity's sake. I am the
Lord's Anointed.

CARLTON HOUSE

WARREN *crosses the stage as the curtain is pulled back to reveal the*
next scene with the PRINCE OF WALES *entertaining his friends.*
SHERIDAN *and* BURKE *are studying a list of MPs,* BURKE *totally*
abstracted from his surroundings.

WARREN: And then Baker examined him and when Baker's back
was turned, the King took the chamberpot and poured it
over his head, saying, 'Now, Sir George, you are a knight of
the chamber.'

DUKE OF YORK: Good for Pa!

PRINCE OF WALES: I must say he's more amusing mad than he
ever was sane.

WARREN: Of course Baker was drenched and also blue.

DUKE OF YORK: Blue?

WARREN: Oh, for some reason his water's blue.

FOOTMAN: Mr Fox, Your Royal Highness.
(FOX *bursts in.*)

PRINCE OF WALES: Charles, Charles. You have returned. But
you have lost flesh.

FOX: Blame that on Mrs Armistead. But what's the news? How is
the King?

PRINCE OF WALES: No change.

FOX: No change? But I've come all this way! I thought he was
dying.

DUKE OF YORK: So did Warren. Had him dead and buried in the
first fortnight.

PRINCE OF WALES: Warren was a little premature. And he's not dead, thank God.

FOX: But he's not better?

PRINCE OF WALES: No, no, no. Nor likely to be, now that Warren's on the case.

WARREN: No, sir.

FOX: That's good. What about support?

SHERIDAN: I'm gradually picking away at Pitt's men and the uncommitted. We need to win over only a few dozen or so.

PRINCE OF WALES: What I have never understood about you, Sheridan, is that you're a playwright but you think like a money-lender. This isn't how you write your plays?

SHERIDAN: It is rather. At least if I'm sober. There's a tide running our way, but we need to be patient; we shall lose support if we seem in any way over-eager.

FOX: But that's Pitt's game. Wait. Spin it out.

PRINCE OF WALES: That's what I said.

FOX: And we *are* over-eager, dammit. I am. I'm also in debt.

SHERIDAN: Fair-minded men will think us disloyal . . .

PRINCE OF WALES: But you're not disloyal, my dear. How can you be disloyal? You're friends of the Prince of Wales.

FOX: All this talk of tides and slow accumulations. It's a battle. It will be won by speeches.

SHERIDAN: Speeches don't win battles. Battles are won by managing the House.

FOX: And boldness and dash. Pitt will fight on his terms if we let him, but we mustn't. We must hustle him out, and once out he'll never crawl back in.

SHERIDAN: Or only if His Majesty recovers.

PRINCE OF WALES: He isn't going to recover. Warren says so.

WARREN: No, sir.

PRINCE OF WALES: There. So, Charles. Trumpets sounding. Colours flying. And less of this accountancy. I'm so glad you're back.

(*They are going.*)

I thought you might have lost your taste for politics in Italy.

DUKE OF YORK: Are there politics in Italy? The only Italians I've come across are hairdressers.

DUNDAS *and* THURLOW *are rallying their supporters and are talking to* SIR SELBY MARKHAM.

DUNDAS: Thank you, Sir Selby. Sir Selby is Member for Worcester. I trust we will see you in the House next week. Mr Pitt would value your support.

SIR SELBY: That depends.

DUNDAS: Sir Selby?

SIR SELBY: This slight indisposition, it does not preclude His Majesty from signing documents?

THURLOW: Why do you ask?

SIR SELBY: My son-in-law is promised a post in the Exchequer. I am told the warrant is drawn up but still awaits His Majesty's signature.

DUNDAS: I am sure Mr Pitt will draw it to His Majesty's attention after the debate next week.

SIR SELBY: Yes.

(*He seems unconvinced and pauses before going out, as if to ask something else, but* DUNDAS *cuts him short.*)

DUNDAS: After the debate, Sir Selby.

SIR SELBY: I am obliged to you. (*Exits.*)

DUNDAS: So, we have that vote for a little while longer. I work it out that we still have a majority of around fifty.

THURLOW: We would have more leeway if our boy was less arctic. Goddammit, why does he not unbend a little? Always on stilts.

FOOTMAN: Sir Boothby Skrymshir.

(SIR BOOTHBY *is a fashionably dressed gentleman, with a vacant nephew,* RAMSDEN.)

DUNDAS: Sir Boothby is Member for Berkshire.

BOOTHBY: My Lord, sir.

DUNDAS: Sir.

BOOTHBY: I received the sad intelligence from my constituency

38

yesterday of the untimely death of Colonel Banstead of the Dragoon Guards.

DUNDAS: My condolences. He will be much missed.

BOOTHBY: The Colonel was, as you know, an unwavering supporter of Mr Pitt and, incidentally, Steward of the Market of Newbury.

DUNDAS: Was he?

BOOTHBY: It occurred to me that you might be in some difficulty in finding a suitable replacement of the calibre of Colonel Banstead, and one name immediately sprang to mind. Ramsden. My nephew.

DUNDAS: That I can fill the vacancy so readily is a great weight off my mind, but I fear your nephew will have to curb his natural eagerness a little while longer.

BOOTHBY: Hear that, Ramsden? Rein it in, Ramsden. Rein it in.

DUNDAS: His Majesty, as you may have heard, is a little indisposed, and is taking a short vacation from his boxes.

BOOTHBY: This indisposition is of some gravity?

DUNDAS: Oh no, no.

THURLOW: He's off-colour, man, that's all.

BOOTHBY: Oh. Then we will take our leave.

DUNDAS: But Mr Pitt can continue to be assured of your support?

BOOTHBY: Oh yes. Other things being equal, of course. Though one mustn't keep Ramsden in suspense.

(*As they leave* PITT *comes in.*)

Sir! (*Bowing to* PITT)

(PITT *is frozen-faced and makes no attempt to acknowledge them.*)

Sir.

(SIR BOOTHBY *leaves, pulling* RAMSDEN *with him, clearly angry at the snub.*)

DUNDAS: That was the Member for Berkshire.

PITT: Yes. What did he want?

THURLOW: He wanted to be spoken to, for a start. Smiled on.

(PITT *says nothing.*)

DUNDAS: He has the nomination for three other seats besides. Four votes in all, William, which we have just lost. It would help our situation if you endeavoured to be less distant. More convivial. It has been known to dine one's supporters.

39

PITT: I am His Majesty's chief minister. I am not running a chop house.

DUNDAS: They gather to the Prince as pus to a boil. When Parliament resumes we will be faced with a group of eloquent and exasperated men.

PITT: Against whom, unless the King recover, no amount of dining will avail. I hate the disorder of it. If only he could sign his name.

THURLOW: We can delay no longer. As Lord Chancellor I must draw up a bill appointing the Prince of Wales Regent. There is no alternative.

PITT: Very well, but take your time.

DUNDAS: For all our sakes. Once it's passed we will be out of a job.

PITT: Meanwhile, before the vote of confidence, Parliament should examine the doctors.

THURLOW: Well then, you will lose the vote. They'll say the King is mad.

PITT: He is not mad. I will not have that word used.

THURLOW: In the House, no – but here, between ourselves, goddammit.

PITT: Here, or in the House, or anywhere. I do not admit the thought.

THURLOW: Then why let the physicians be examined? They will all agree.

PITT: Do you think so? Three doctors, each with his reputation to make, and they will all say the same thing? What if they were lawyers?

THURLOW: Oh, very well. (*Going*) But he is mad, dammit.

DUNDAS: When your father was ill, what form did it take?

PITT: Why? What has that got to do with it? My father was mad, that was the form it took. (*Pause.*) But not this form. Not this form at all.

(PITT *gathers up his papers, crosses the stage where the curtain is pulled back to reveal* FITZROY.)

FITZROY: He soils his clothes. Urine. Excrement. He talks filth, the slops of his mind swilling over. I am not a nurse. If His Majesty cannot regulate himself how should he regulate the country?

PAGES: Sharp! Sharp! The King! The King!

FITZROY: I shall be relieved when it is ended . . . one way or another.

(*The* PAGES *come in with the writing kit, followed by* GREVILLE *and the* KING.)

KING: Yes?

FITZROY: It's Mr Pitt, sir.

KING: Where?

PITT: Here, Your Majesty.

KING: Stand close, Mr Pitt. You'll have to speak up, I don't see very well. There is a fog here and in my ears-ears-ears-ears . . .

(*I have tried to suggest the* KING's *tendency to get stuck on a word or syllable, a juddering form of utterance that he cannot control except by speaking very fast.*)

You drink-drink-drink-drink. I smell it on your breath. Still a young man-man-man. No-no-no. I know-know-know . . .

(*He stumbles.*)

PITT: Would Your Majesty not prefer to sit?

KING: Stand-stand-stand. Can't sit-sit-sit shit-shit-shit . . .

(PITT *looks at* FITZROY, *who is aloof.* GREVILLE, *always the more humane equerry, intervenes.*)

GREVILLE: Sir!

(*This stops the* KING.)

You must interrupt His Majesty. It is the only way.

PITT: I saw Your Majesty last week. I left some urgent papers.

KING: Yes. Remember, remember. Remember you. Little boy. Father old. Mad once. Not mad, though, me. Not mad-mad-mad-mad. Madjesty majesty. Majust just nerves nerves nerves sss. (*He hisses into silence, but every silence costs him an immense effort, shaken as he is by unspoken speech.*)

PITT: Yes, sir. It will pass.

(PITT *hands the* KING *a paper but it goes unread and unremarked*.)

Parliament resumes tomorrow, sir.

KING: Parliament, Parliament . . . Do nothing nothing nothing nothing Pitt Pitt Pitt do – nothing nothing. I am not mad mad mad . . . Can't see can't see mist mist missed Queen missed her, oh missed her Queen, gone gone gone . . .

PITT: The doctors thought it best, sir.

KING: (*Instantly more agitated*) Doc doc doc doctors doctortures doctoremnetors doctalk doctalk talk talk talk talk . . .

(*The* KING *is howling helplessly, and he seizes* GREVILLE's *hand and puts it over his mouth. He is perhaps shitting himself too, because as* GREVILLE *helps him out of the room the* KING *clutches his dressing-gown behind him, a despairing and incontinent wretch. The* PAGES *and* FITZROY *follow expressionless as* PITT, *plainly shaken by the spectacle, puts down his papers; but as he is found by the spotlight, now addressing the House of Commons, he has recovered his composure and smoothly lies about his visit.*)

WESTMINSTER

PITT: Honourable members would, I am sure, like to know that I saw His Majesty yesterday, that he was pleased to see me, we discussed the recall of the House, and the only symptom of his disorder was a tendency to repeat himself and a wandering from one topic to another . . . a characteristic that is shared by most of the converse of polite society, which if judged severely would warrant the consignment to Bedlam of many in this House. (*Laughter.*)

(PITT *turns, the wall splits and pulls back to reveal the Speaker's chair and the table with the mace and the despatch box at which* PITT *finishes his speech.*)

However, since honourable members would, I'm sure, wish to satisfy themselves on the state of His Majesty's health, his physicians are to be examined by a committee of the House.

SPEAKER: Mr Fox.

FOX: It is all very well to examine the doctors but the more pressing matter, should His Majesty's indisposition prove not to be temporary . . .

(*Uproar; shouting above it*) . . . should the indisposition prove not to be temporary, is the situation of His Royal Highness the Prince of Wales. (*Shouts of 'Not now!' 'Too soon!' 'Leave it' 'Leave that!'*)

WESTMINSTER

The scene changes to a committee room where WARREN *is addressing the Committee, chaired by* PITT *and attended by* DUNDAS, SHERIDAN, BURKE *and* FOX.

WARREN: So, whilst His Majesty is in a special situation, comparison with similar cases that I have treated over many years leads me to conclude that His Majesty is suffering from a persistent, and to my mind, incurable delirium.

PITT: So, you are all agreed that His Majesty is suffering from delirium?

BAKER: Yes.

PEPYS: Yes.

PITT: Dr Warren?

WARREN: Yes. Yes.

FOX: So, we have a unanimous verdict. The King is suffering from delirium. What else is there to say?

BAKER: Ah, but that is delirium without fever. It began as delirium with fever.

PEPYS: *Delirium cum febri* –

BAKER: It is now delirium without fever.

PEPYS: *Delirium sine febri.*

WARREN: It makes no difference.

BAKER: I think it does. The pulse sometimes rises to 110.

WARREN: The pulse has nothing to do with it.

BAKER: I beg to differ.

PITT: So you do not seem to be in agreement at all. Mr Fox.

FOX: What form does the delirium take?

WARREN: Sheer raving.

43

BAKER: I disagree. Sometimes His Majesty makes good sense.

PITT: Sir Lucas.

PEPYS: I'm inclined to agree with Warren.

BAKER: Oh!

PEPYS: But what Baker says is true also. I will say this. His Majesty is in perfect command of his bowels. True, there have been unfortunate accidents, but that can be put down to the emetics that are being introduced into his food.

DUNDAS: Can you at least agree on what the disease is called?

BAKER: Flying gout.

PEPYS: Rheumatism in the head.

WARREN: Simple dementia.

BURKE: And when will His Majesty recover?

(*Silence.*)

DUNDAS: Flying gout, creeping palsy or galloping consumption, how long?

WARREN: Never.

PEPYS: A year, two years.

BAKER: It might be quite soon. There are larger considerations. This Committee seeks to know what is wrong with His Majesty. I say look to the country. It is rich, prosperous. Smiling villages, brisk little towns, teeming cities. What is wrong with that, you say? This: the greater the progress the greater the sickness. And why? Because of leisure, because of idleness, because of money to spare. That is what breeds this melancholy from which His Majesty is suffering. Leisure, prosperity, civilization.

FOX: But when will he recover? This year, next year, sometime, never? Doctors, you might as well count cherry stones.

PITT: Thank you, gentlemen.

(*The Committee breaks up.* PITT *left alone.* DUNDAS *comes in with a paper which he gives to* PITT.)

DUNDAS: A majority of thirty.

PITT: Thirty.

DUNDAS: At least we have more time.

PITT: Not enough. I saw the King again this afternoon. He did not know me. I was mistaken. He is mad. The next vote will not be so easy. We are finished.

44

PITT *alone*.

LADY PEMBROKE *floats in*.

LADY PEMBROKE: Mr Pitt.

PITT: (*Sharply*) Yes? Forgive me. Lady Pembroke.

LADY PEMBROKE: Mr Pitt, you are, I understand, dissatisfied
with His Majesty's doctors?
(PITT *nods*.)
Mr Pitt. My mother-in-law lost her wits, and a succession of
physicians failed to recover them for her. However, there
was one doctor who was confident of her return to health,
and accordingly she was placed in his care.

PITT: And is she recovered?

LADY PEMBROKE: Entirely. Rides to hounds. Founded some
almshouses. Embroiders round the clock. I have written
down his name.
(*She floats away. The curtains are drawn back to reveal the full
stage as* FORTNUM *announces* DR WILLIS.)

FOOTMAN: Dr Willis.
(WILLIS *is a homely provincial figure and looks less like a doctor
– which he is – than a clergyman – which he also is*.)

PITT: (*With a paper*) Your name has been given me by Lady
Pembroke as one of particular skill in the treatment of
intellectual maladies. You cured her mother-in-law. You
were a clergyman but now run an asylum in Lincolnshire.

WILLIS: I prefer to call it a farm, sir. My patients occupy
themselves in manual work and activities connected with the
estate.

PITT: Quite so. Though in His Majesty's case manual work would
hardly be appropriate. You have studied the reports on His
Majesty's condition?

WILLIS: Yes. Interesting and very puzzling.
(WILLIS *has the reports, which he goes through*.)
No evidence of earlier attacks. No family history. And yet we
have all these symptoms.

PITT: Yes.

WILLIS: Skin tender. Pains in the lower limbs. Talks

continuously with varying degrees of sense.

PITT: Well?

WILLIS: And variously diagnosed. Ossification of the membrane. Rheumatism in the head. Flying gout. Oh dear me. Delirium with fever. Delirium without fever. Hard to say what it is. Can't even give it a name. Puzzling, very puzzling. No, I'm bound to say I've never come across a condition quite like this before.

PITT: But I was told you were experienced in these disorders.

WILLIS: I am.

PITT: Yet you've never come across anything like this before?

WILLIS: No.

PITT: In which case I was misled as to your abilities, Dr Willis.

WILLIS: (*Unoffended*) These intellectual maladies present themselves in a bewildering variety. I am always interested to see a new one.

PITT: Interested, sir? This is not an object of interest. This is His Majesty the King. I did not fetch you down from Lincolnshire just to indulge your idle curiosity.

WILLIS: Oh, it is not idle.

PITT: I was given to understand you might be able to cure His Majesty. It seems I was misled. Good afternoon, sir.

WILLIS: Oh, I can cure him. I'm just not sure what from.

PITT: Are you certain?

WILLIS: What about?

PITT: The cure, man.

WILLIS: Oh, no doubt about that.

PITT: When? How long?

WILLIS: Hard to say, but sooner rather than later, and provided I have certain undertakings. Authority over the patient. Access to him at all times.

(*The* QUEEN, *who has been listening at the door, bursts in, pursued by* LADY PEMBROKE.)

QUEEN: No, no. I must speak, I must speak.

PITT: Dr Willis, madam.

WILLIS: Your Majesty.

QUEEN: Have you met His Majesty?

WILLIS: No, ma'am.

46

QUEEN: It is the same with all the doctors. None of them know him. He is not himself. So how can they restore him to his proper self, not knowing what that self is? Where do they look for it? The King is not mad. He is an angel of kindness and goodness.

LADY PEMBROKE: (*Anxious lest they be discovered in the King's apartments*) Ma'am.

PITT: You should also be aware, Dr Willis, that there are physicians in attendance who do not think His Majesty will recover.

QUEEN: And who are not anxious that he should recover.

WILLIS: He will recover, ma'am. I promise you.

(*The* QUEEN *and* LADY PEMBROKE *leave.*)

WILLIS: Kind or not, the King will have to be curbed in the hope that he will learn to curb himself.

PITT: In the *hope*, sir. You said you were certain.

WILLIS: I am, sir.

PITT: Well let us have no more talk of hope. And you must show the same optimism to Parliament as you have done with me. The survival of the Government depends upon it. Your certainty, Dr Willis, is *my* hope. My only hope.

(GREVILLE *enters.*)

This is Captain Greville, the King's equerry. Good day, Dr Willis. (*Leaves.*)

GREVILLE: Dr Willis, Mr Pitt is anxious that the King should recover because his Government depends on it. I am anxious that the King recover, but that is because I love His Majesty. Before you meet him I should tell you that his manner is unusual. Abrupt, spasmodic, so that what might seem odd in an ordinary person, in him is normal, just his way.

WILLIS: The state of monarchy and the state of lunacy share a frontier. Some of my lunatics fancy themselves kings. He is King, so where shall his fancy take refuge?

GREVILLE: We do not use the word lunatic, sir, in relation to His Majesty.

WILLIS: Who is to say what is normal in a king? Deferred to, agreed with, acquiesced in. Who could flourish on such a daily diet of compliance? To be curbed, stood up to, in a

47

word thwarted, exercises the character, elasticates the spirit, makes it pliant. It is the want of such exercise that makes rulers rigid. So we must begin by giving him that exercise as we would exercise a horse, and break him as we would break a horse.

GREVILLE: This is not some creature taught to show paces like a managed filly. This is the King.

WILLIS: Whom I must cure.

('Sharp! Sharp! The King! The King!' *and a babble of talk in the corridor announces the imminent arrival of the* KING.)

GREVILLE: One feature of His Majesty's disorder was that having arrived at a word he found himself unable to leave it. That seems to be passing and now he simply talks without ceasing – yesterday four hours at a stretch. You must not be bound by etiquette – interrupt him.

WILLIS: Etiquette? Never fear, Mr . . . Greville? . . . I am a doctor. I am not here to make myself agreeable.

(*Accompanied by* FITZROY, PAPANDIEK *and* BRAUN, *the* KING *comes on, talking all the time, very fast and without pause. His legs are bandaged and a stained cloth is tied round his middle like a nappy. Nevertheless he is still wearing the ribbon of the Garter. He slowly circles* WILLIS, *looking at him keenly but with no change in his tone.*)

KING: (*The speech begins offstage*) Talking of land we saw the sea first when we were thirty-five. Five sevens are thirty-five, five eights are forty. We had been told it was blue, all the poets said it was blue, we read, we read, read, read, read it was blue, blue, and it wasn't blue, blue at all, grey, grey, grey. Weren't we disappointed, it's like everything else, you go see for yourself and it's not the case at all. Sea not blue more of I don't know what colour it was when we went in, sea bathing, we couldn't bathe now. No. The water would soak into our skin. We leak. There are holes in our skin. We take in water. We would sink, founder. The doctors have made more holes so we would go to the bottom in an instant. We can plough a furrow, you know, give us a field, a decent plough and we could plough you a furrow as straight as a ruler, straight as a ruler done by a ruler, and another beside

48

it and another beside that until you had as pretty a
ploughed field as you could find this side of Cirencester.
Put us out of our kingdom tomorrow and I would not want
for employment.

WILLIS: I have a farm.

KING: Give me the management of fifty acres and ploughing and
sowing and harvest, and I could do it and make me a
handsome profit into the bargain.

WILLIS: I said I have a farm, Your Majesty.
(*The* KING *stops, looks at him.*)

GREVILLE: This gentleman, sir, has made the illness under
which Your Majesty labours his special study.

WILLIS: (*To* GREVILLE) Hush, sir.

KING: A mad doctor, is it? I am not mad, just nervous.

WILLIS: I will endeavour to alleviate some of the inconveniences
from which Your Majesty suffers.

KING: Inconveniences? Insults. Assaults. And salts beside
rubbed into these wounds, sir. See.
(WILLIS *loosens the bandage to look at the sores on his legs.*)
I eat my meals with a spoon, sir. A pusher. George by the
Grace of God King of England, Ireland, Scotland, Elector
of Hanover, Duke of Brunswick. A pusher. By your dress,
sir, and general demeanour I would say you were a minister
of God.

WILLIS: That is true, Your Majesty. I was once in the service of
the Church, now I practise medicine.

KING: Then I am sorry for it. You have quitted a profession I
have always loved, and embraced one I most heartily detest.

WILLIS: Our Saviour went about healing the sick.

KING: Yes, but he had not £700 a year for it.
(GREVILLE *and the* PAGES *laugh.* WILLIS *does not laugh.*)
Yes, but he had not £700 a year for it, eh? Not bad for a
madman.

WILLIS: I have a hospital in Lincolnshire, sir.

KING: I know Lincolnshire. Fine sheep. Admirable sheep.
There are pigs, too. Pigs can be very fine. Hay is the means
of maintenance of the cow, grass of the sheep, oats of the
horse, and pigs will eat anything. I have a fondness for pigs.

49

But I know of no hospitals.

WILLIS: We have cows and sheep and pigs also.

KING: In the hospital? Are they mad too?

WILLIS: My patients work, sir. They till the soil. They cultivate and in so doing they acquire a better conceit of themselves.

KING: I am King of England, sir. A man can have no better conceit of himself than that.

(WILLIS *suddenly takes hold of the* KING's *shoulder, and the* KING *freezes.* FITZROY, GREVILLE *and the pages are plainly shocked and the* KING *rigid with anger.* WILLIS *deliberately looks the* KING *in the eye.*)

Do you look at me, sir?

WILLIS: I do, sir.

KING: I have you in my eye.

WILLIS: No. I have you in my eye.

KING: You are bold, but by God I am bolder.

(*The* KING *suddenly goes for* WILLIS *but* WILLIS *dodges and the force of the rush makes the* KING *fall down. He remains sitting on the ground, while* WILLIS *lectures him.*)

WILLIS: You can control your utterance, sir, if you would. I believe you can be well if only you will.

KING: Do not look at me. I am not one of your farmers.

WILLIS: Your Majesty must behave, or endeavour to do so.

KING: (*Still struggling*) Must, must? Whose must? Your must or my must? No must. Get away from me, you scabby bumsucker.

PAPANDIEK: Easy sir, easy.

KING: (*As they try to get him up*) No, no. Leave me, boys. Let me sit upon the ground and tell . . . tell-tell-tell-tell . . . tell this lump-headed fool to shut his gob box. You spunk-splasher, you Lincolnshire lickfingers . . .

WILLIS: Clean your tongue, sir. Clean your tongue.

GREVILLE: Hush, sir.

PAPANDIEK: Be still, sir.

KING: I will not be still. I will be a guest in the graveyard first.

BRAUN: Go easy, my old love.

PAPANDIEK: Steady, Your Majesty, steady. Leave off, leave off.

WILLIS: Very well. If Your Majesty does not behave, you must be restrained.

(WILLIS *opens the door and three of his servants, grim-faced and in leather aprons, wheel in the restraining chair, a wooden contraption with clamps for the arms and legs and a band for the head. The sight of the restraining chair momentarily silences the* KING.)

KING: When felons were induced to talk they were first shown the instrument of their torture. The King is shown the instrument of his to induce him not to talk. Well, I won't, I won't. Not for you and all your ding boys.
(*The* KING *begins abusing them again, with a torrent of obscenity, as, quietly as first, but growing louder as the scene comes to its climax, we hear Handel's Coronation Anthem,* Zadok the Priest. *One servant thrusts aside the protesting* PAGES *while the other two lift the* KING *up and amid the ensuing pandemonium manhandle him into the restraining chair.*)
You clap-ridden shit-sack. See them off boys! See them off!
(*As he is hauled to the chair*) Goddam you. I'll have you all thrashed for this! Horse-whipped. Lie off, you rascals. Lie off.

FITZROY: This is unseemly, sir. Who are these bully boys?

GREVILLE: You have no business, sir. His Majesty is ill.

FITZROY: I must inform His Royal Highness. This is a scandal.

GREVILLE: Call off your dogs, sir. Who are these barkers?

WILLIS: If the King refuses food he will be restrained. If he claims to have no appetite he will be restrained. If he swears and indulges in meaningless discourse he will be restrained. If he throws off his bedclothes, tears away his bandages, scratches at his sores, and if he does not strive every day and always towards his own recovery, then he must be restrained.
(*Willis's men stand back from the* KING *and we see that he has been strapped into the chair, feet and arms clamped, his head held rigid by a band round his forehead.*)

KING: (*Howling*) I am the King of England.

WILLIS: No, sir. You are the patient.
(*The Coronation Anthem finally reaches its climax and bursts forth in the chorus of* Zadok the Priest, *as the* KING *struggles, howling, in the chair, with Willis's men lined up behind him.*

FORTNUM *slips in with the chamber pot. He holds it up for examination by the unheeding* FITZROY, *his shadow big upon the wall, the music still at full volume as the curtain falls.*)

PART 2

WINDSOR

The physicians' table, laden with all their medical paraphernalia.
WARREN *and* BAKER *enter.*

BAKER: No, no. You have not understood the arrangements.

WARREN: I understand the arrangements perfectly well. Can't you see how clever he's been?

BAKER: We are all to be consulted. You and I arrive at eleven, discuss the day's treatment with Willis, then share a rota for the rest of the day.

WARREN: Exactly. But Willis is in residence here at Windsor, whereas we spend half our time on the road from London. So whereas we are in attendance part of the day, Willis has access to the King at any time and can give him what treatment he chooses. The Prince don't like it either.

BAKER: I wouldn't want to upset His Royal Highness.

WARREN: Besides, Willis is not a member of the Royal College of Physicians. He's drab, provincial and unconnected. But I tell you, we would do well to speak with one voice, or he will displace us all. Look at you, George. The King's first physician. For how long, I wonder?

BAKER: I hadn't thought of that.

WARREN: And another thing. You and I, George . . . we may be a trifle old-fashioned, but we are both skilled in the practice of all-round medicine. Present us with any of the body's multifarious ailments, and we can diagnose and treat.

BAKER: We're general practitioners.

WARREN: Exactly. But Willis isn't. Willis specializes. You and I, George, we treat the whole man. Willis confines himself to the understanding, the intellectual parts, the head. Well, what sort of medicine is that?

BAKER: It's profitable medicine. And if you've got a madhouse like Willis, there's all the board and lodging money as well.

WARREN: But isn't it narrow? Circumscribed? The body colonized, divided up . . . one man's empire the stomach, another the supreme authority where joints are concerned. That isn't the general physic we were taught, is it? We'll have to be careful, George, because if that sort of partial medicine catches on, we're finished, you and I. A general physician will be a poor man's physician.

(PEPYS *bustles in with something hidden behind his back.*)

PEPYS: Good news!

(*He brings it out with a flourish. It is a bedpan covered with a towel, which he removes like a conjuror as he thrusts the bedpan under* WARREN'*s nose.*)

A fetid and a stinking stool! The colour good, well-shaped and a prodigious quantity.

WARREN: Pepys. I am saying to Baker there must be a firm alliance between us against this interloper.

PEPYS: Quite so. Quite so. Mind you, the urine is a little dark. Or is it the light?

BRAUN: Doctor Willis.

(WILLIS *enters with* GREVILLE.)

WARREN: One voice, remember.

WILLIS: Sir George. I understand we are to issue a daily bulletin as to His Majesty's condition.

BAKER: Perhaps. But then perhaps not. I don't know what you've been given to understand, I'm sure.

WILLIS: I have prepared one if you would care to look it over.

WARREN: (*Snatching it*) We were not meant to look this over. We were meant to draw this up together. 'A good night's sleep'? The pages say he never slept for more than an hour together.

BAKER: And there's no mention of the pulse.

PEPYS: Or the stool.

WARREN: It's a concoction. (*He screws it up.*) It must be rewritten. Now. The Privy Council says we must decide on treatment together. What's your suggestion, Willis? More damned lectures, I suppose.

WILLIS: I talk to His Majesty in order to recall him to a proper sense of himself.

WARREN: Talk. Baker?

BAKER: As his pulse is quite steady, now might be the moment for some more James's Powders. A good sweat never did

anybody any harm. And some musk, I think, though the
stench is so obnoxious he may not be able to keep it down –
though that may be a good thing, too. Yes, a good spew and a
good sweat.

WARREN: Pepys?

PEPYS: I prefer to come at it from the other direction. If one
purgative produces such a prodigious quantity as this, I'd be
a fool not to double the dose.

WARREN: My instinct is to apply more blisters to the legs, then
shave his head and apply them there.

WILLIS: His legs are still suppurating from your last course of
blisters.

WARREN: Of course they are. That is the point of them, *doctor*.
The poison is finding its way out through the legs. So,
Willis's talk, Baker's sweats, Pepys's purge or my blisters.
Which is it to be?

BAKER: I think all of them: Yes? After all, one of us must have it
right. Prepare the blisters.
(BRAUN *goes off*.)

GREVILLE: May I beg you not to blister His Majesty's head, sir.
(*The doctors look askance at this interference*.)
His skin is so tender he cannot even bear his wig.

WARREN: Good. That will make it all the more efficacious.
(FORTNUM *comes on and whispers to* GREVILLE.)

GREVILLE: His Majesty has just been sick.

WARREN: Yes. That will be the emetic I introduced into his
gruel. No need for all that food festering in his insides. One
last thing. I am of the opinion that His Majesty would benefit
were he to be lodged nearer London . . . at the Palace at
Kew, for instance.

PEPYS: Oh yes, Kew would be much handier for me.

GREVILLE: His Majesty is fond of Windsor.

WARREN: What has that got to do with it?

GREVILLE: Will not the familiarity of his surroundings assist in
his recovery?

BAKER: If it did, you would not know it. You're not a doctor.

WARREN: A change of scene might be just the ticket. Willis. You
have no objection?

WILLIS: It's all one to me. I would have him in Lincolnshire if I had my way. He would be on the mend there in no time.

(WARREN, BAKER *and* PEPYS *leave, as, sitting but not fastened in the chair of restraint, the* KING *is wheeled in by* PAPANDIEK. *The* KING *still holds the bowl in which he has been sick and as he wipes the* KING'*s face with a cloth,* GREVILLE *calls for* FITZROY *to assist, but* FITZROY *remains aloof.*)

GREVILLE: Captain Fitzroy. Captain Fitzroy.

(PAPANDIEK *attends to the* KING *while* GREVILLE *takes* FITZROY *aside.*)

FITZROY: I will not handle the King, sir. I cannot do it.

GREVILLE: Fitzroy, please.

FITZROY: Sir, it is not my function.

GREVILLE: Is it the treatment?

FITZROY: Hang the treatment. My function is to frame the monarch for public view. I am the lens, sir. I am to do with appearances. My function is to expurgate his humanity, expunge all that is common, and present him as an object fit for public veneration. With this? I will attend, but no more.

(*During this exchange between* GREVILLE *and* FITZROY *the* KING *has been chattering away to himself, the first part of his monologue largely inaudible to the audience, but the last part (from* 'This is the English way') *clearly heard.*)

KING: Oh God, please restore me to my senses, or let me die directly, for Thy Mercy's sake. Thrown in the chair, enthroned in the chair, the chair a machine for punishing, a fastening chair, a fasten-in chair, a fashioning chair to fashion the King to the ordinary fashion. To fashion the King to the ordinary passion. This is the English way. This is how they would have their kings. This is the Glorious Revolution. A king in shackles. They would have all their kings mad in England. It is convenient.

(BRAUN *wheels in the trolley with the burners and glasses and dons the gloves ready for the blistering.*)

What's this? What's this? The hot cups? No, please. I beg you. I have been scal-scal-scalded enough.

BRAUN: Sorry, sir. Doctor's orders.

(*The* KING *begins to say the General Confession here set out in full though the blistering will cut it short.*)

KING: Almighty and most merciful Father, we have erred and
strayed from thy ways like lost sheep. We have followed too
much the devices and desires of our hearts. We have
offended against thy holy laws; we have left undone the
things we ought to have done and we have done the things we
ought not to have done and there is no health in us. But thou,
O God, have mercy upon us, miserable offenders, spare thou
them that confess their faults, restore thou them that are
penitent according to thy promises declared unto mankind in
Christ Jesus our Lord.

(PAPANDIEK, *wincing, holds the* KING's *head while* BRAUN
with obvious relish applies the blistering glass to the KING's
forehead.)

No, oh oh, mercy. Oh my God. No, no. (*He screams as*
BRAUN *takes a second glass.*)

WILLIS: Leave it, leave it.

BRAUN: But I've scarcely started, sir.

(*He manages to put another blister with more screams from the*
KING *before* GREVILLE *stops him.*)

WILLIS: I don't care whether you've started or finished. Stop, I
say. The treatment does not signify.

KING: Oh, thank God. Thank God.

WILLIS: Thank God, yes, sir. But also thank me.

KING: Thank you, sir? No, sir. You are a fiend.

WILLIS: Dry His Majesty's head.

(*Gently* PAPANDIEK *does so, the* KING *moaning to himself.*)

GREVILLE: Have you no faith in these treatments?

WILLIS: They will not cure him.

GREVILLE: So why permit them?

WILLIS: My colleagues have prescribed them. Besides, if His
Majesty perceives that it is in my power to remit them, or cut
them short, they are not without value.

GREVILLE: Then that is torture.

WILLIS: Medicine, young man . . . my medicine . . . is
mastery. When I stop the blistering, the King is grateful
and he perceives my authority, and thus he will come to
obey me.

KING: I had an empire once. There were forests there and lakes and plains and little soft hills.

PAPANDIEK: Leave off, sir. The doctor says you ain't to talk of America.

KING: Monarch and master, I have carried my eager hands to every part of that smiling land, but wherever I have laid my loving hand my touch has raised mutiny.

GREVILLE: Be still sir. Hush, I beg you.

KING: The snowy paps are all inflamed, all nature in a turmoil.

BRAUN: It ain't America. It's Lady P.

KING: But with tact and love I shall take her hand and carry it to my sceptre, to let her feel its strength and its softness.
(PAPANDIEK *tries to hush the* KING.)

BRAUN: (*To* WILLIS) It's America or it's Her Ladyship, sir, one or the other, but it shouldn't be either, should it, sir?

WILLIS: These fancies are improper, sir. You have been told before. I see you, sir.

KING: No, sir. You do not see me. Nobody sees me. I am not here.

WILLIS: I have you in my eye, sir, and I shall keep you in my eye until you begin to behave and do as you are told.

KING: I am the King. I tell. I am not told. I am the verb, sir. I am not the object.

WILLIS: Until you can govern yourself you are not fit to govern others, and until you do I shall govern you.

KING: Govern yourself then, you goat. An old fumbling fellow like you tupping the Queen. Where is she? What have you done with her?

WILLIS: Have a care, sir, or I shall have you blistered again.

KING: Where is she? Have you taken her to Lincolnshire to your colony? Is she ploughing, sir, with the others, or are you ploughing her?

WILLIS: Fetch the waistcoat.

KING: Is she dead? Has he killed her? Show me the Queen. Show me.

WILLIS: The Queen is not dead, sir. And if you behave yourself and do as I tell you, then the Queen shall come to Kew and you shall see her.

KING: Kew, what's this?

BRAUN: We're going to Kew, sir.

KING: Kew? What for? I'd as soon go to Japan. And the other one, the other one. Shall I see her?

(FORTNUM *returns, seemingly wearing the straitwaistcoat, though it is in fact inside out.*)

WILLIS: No, sir. You will not see her. And you will not speak of her.

KING: Elizabeth, shall I see her? I must speak of her. I love her . . . I love her . . .

WILLIS: Fasten the waistcoat, fasten the waistcoat.

(FORTNUM *grasps the* KING's *hands, and* BRAUN *and* PAPANDIEK *pull the waistcoat off* FORTNUM's *outstretched arms and on to the* KING's, *so that he is now wearing the waistcoat the right way out.*)

KING: Then I am dead. I am a coffin king. I will be murdered: taken out and my genitals torn off and pulled apart by horses and my limbs exhibited in a neighbouring town. I am here, Doctor Willis, but I am not all there.

(*The last glimpse of the* KING *before the curtain is drawn is of* BRAUN *with his foot in the small of the* KING's *back, pulling the straps tight.*)

CARLTON HOUSE

When the curtain is pulled back on Carlton House we find the PRINCE OF WALES *in a similar situation, his servant with his foot in the small of the* PRINCE's *back fastening him into a corset, prior to having his portrait painted.*

PRINCE OF WALES: No, no, please. It is torture. What a terrible garment.

DUKE OF YORK: Courage, Prin.

PRINCE OF WALES: No. Let me breathe.

(*They stop the lacing.*)

SHERIDAN: When Parliament declares Your Highness Regent, Pitt will endeavour to impose restraints.

PRINCE OF WALES: Restraints? What sort of restraints? I want no restraints. Go on. Go on.

(*The lacing begins again.*)
Restraints, what on?

SHERIDAN: Your freedom to make appointments.

PRINCE OF WALES: But if I can't give anyone jobs, who will support me anyway?

SHERIDAN: That is the purpose of it. To tie your hands.

PRINCE OF WALES: Tie my hands?

DUKE OF YORK: I say, that's not fair. Can the fellow do that?

BURKE: It's hard to say what he can and can't do. There is no exact precedent. Of course the Revolution of 1688 established the principle that . . .

FOX: Oh, do be quiet. This is politics, not principle.

PRINCE OF WALES: The King's hands were never tied, so why mine? I'm not having it.

FOX: There can be no question of it. When you are declared Regent it must be with full powers to dismiss Pitt and appoint . . . whomsoever you choose in his place.

BURKE: Charles!

FOX: Of course as Whigs we've always maintained the opposite, that the power of the Crown *should* be restrained, but these are extraordinary circumstances.

PRINCE OF WALES: They are. I'm a good fellow, for a start. My father wasn't . . . isn't. And I'm a Whig too and for the best of reasons. My father ruled me like he did the Bostonians, and now this is my tea-party. Restrictions indeed.
(HOPPNER *has wheeled out a vaulting horse, which the* PRINCE *now ascends.* HOPPNER *hands him a sword and poses him in a suitably warlike posture, ready for the portrait.*)
Now, Mr Hoppner. I am all yours. Noble thoughts. Noble thoughts.

FOOTMAN: Sir Boothby Skrymshir and Mr Ramsden Skrymshir, Your Royal Highness.

SHERIDAN: Ah, Sir Boothby.

BOOTHBY: Your Royal Highness.

PRINCE OF WALES: Sir.

SHERIDAN: Sir Boothby is here to commiserate with Your Royal Highness on the continuing indisposition of His Majesty.

PRINCE OF WALES: Much touched, much touched.

BOOTHBY: How is His Majesty's indisposition?

PRINCE OF WALES: It continues. It continues.

BOOTHBY: My nephew Ramsden has been utterly disconsolate, his spirits only sustained by Your Royal Highness's own resplendent health and the amplification of your prospects.

PRINCE OF WALES: So kind.

BOOTHBY: In the event of . . . in any event, my nephew is most anxious to serve Your Royal Highness in any capacity whatsoever, but in particular as the Steward of the Market of Newbury.

PRINCE OF WALES: Sheridan? We do not wish to be painted thinking of the market of Newbury.

SHERIDAN: It does stand vacant at the moment, sir.

DUKE OF YORK: Steward of the market of where?

RAMSDEN: Dewsbury.

BOOTHBY: Newbury, Ramsden.

DUKE OF YORK: I'm Bishop of Osnabruck, you know. Keen on sheep, are you?

BOOTHBY: A childhood dream, sir.

PRINCE OF WALES: We are touched by your solicitude, sir, and when the time comes we shall remember.

BOOTHBY: Sir. Bow, Ramsden. (*They are going out.*) Backwards, Ramsden, backwards.

SHERIDAN: And I am most grateful to you.

FOX: Grateful! To that booby?

PRINCE OF WALES: Ludicrous fellow.

SHERIDAN: Perhaps. But his vote is not ludicrous, nor the three other votes he brings with him. It is on him and other such marketable flotsam we depend. So that's four more.
(SHERIDAN *goes back to the wallchart on which he is ticking off the* PRINCE's *parliamentary supporters.*)

DUKE OF YORK: (*Looking at the canvas*) I say, that's awfully good. Fellow's got you to a T.

PRINCE OF WALES: Mr Hoppner. If, looking ahead . . . if my circumstances were to alter, would you . . . could you preserve the face while adapting . . . the robes, say?

HOPPNER: That is easily arranged, sir. I generally get someone in to do the drapery in any event.

FOX: Oh, so you're one of those face painters, are you?

HOPPNER: Not exclusively.

FOX: Face painters, body painters, drapery painters . . . it's not art, it's manufacture.

PRINCE OF WALES: Painting has always been manufacture. There can be button painters for all I care.

HOPPNER: There are, sir. Buttons and lace.

FOX: So. You get better and better at doing less and less. What a world!

PRINCE OF WALES: That just shows, Charles, under all your radical talk, how old-fashioned you are.

FOOTMAN: Captain Fitzroy, Your Royal Higness.

(FITZROY *has come in.*)

PRINCE OF WALES: Ah, Fitzroy. How is our invalid?

FITZROY: Raving this morning, sir; in the straitjacket this afternoon.

PRINCE OF WALES: Oh dear.

DUKE OF YORK: New man not doing the trick then?

FITZROY: No, sir.

PRINCE OF WALES: Oh, what a shame. Still. Noble thoughts. Noble thoughts.

(FITZROY *takes* SHERIDAN *aside but* FOX *overhears.*)

FITZROY: I have come with Lord Thurlow.

FOX: That brute? What for?

SHERIDAN: Lord Thurlow is here, sir.

PRINCE OF WALES: Excellent, excellent. Fetch him in.

FOX: This is your spy, I suppose. Why didn't you tell me?

SHERIDAN: There is no party without obnoxious persons. He has never been on the wrong side.

FOX: I will not serve with him. He hasn't got a Whig breath in his body.

SHERIDAN: Charles. You cannot undo weeks of calculation by a fit of pique.

FITZROY: Lord Thurlow, sir.

THURLOW: Your Royal Highness.

PRINCE OF WALES: Lord Thurlow.

THURLOW: I can tell you in confidence that Mr Pitt is so despondent that he is preparing to return to private practice as a barrister.

SHERIDAN: So, he's giving up. That's worth knowing.

FOX: It is, only I read it in the newspaper this morning. How are we to recompense you for this invaluable intelligence and for your . . . defection?

THURLOW: Defection, no. Administrations come and go. As I see it, the function of the Lord Chancellor is to provide continuity.

BURKE: There are precedents which would justify that, particularly if we go back to . . .

FOX: What's your price?

THURLOW: To remain on the Woolsack.

PRINCE OF WALES: You shall, I promise you.

THURLOW: Thank you, sir, and were I to offer advice I would say that the present situation calls for the utmost delicacy.

PRINCE OF WALES: Oh yes. Quite agree. The utmost.

THURLOW: Everything will come to you in due course. Your Highness has but to wait . . .

PRINCE OF WALES: Wait! Wait! My life has been waiting. I want to be doing not dangling. I endeavour to cultivate languor, but it is hard to be languid when the throne of England is pending. To be heir to the throne is not a position; it is a predicament. People laugh at me. What must I do to be taken seriously? I tell you, sir, to be Prince of Wales is not becoming to a gentleman.

(FOX, DUKE OF YORK, FITZROY, *all leave with the* PRINCE OF WALES *as* HOPPNER *cleans up*.)

THURLOW: Yes. It takes character to withstand the rigours of indolence. Do we need Fox?

SHERIDAN: We need the Prince and they come as a set. But I know what you mean. Fox despises me because I trim and count heads. He is the great Whig, you see, and I just the manager. Still, I must put up with that, for his friends will vote with him though he coalesce with the devil. But it's fiddling work.

THURLOW: Why do you not stick to the theatre?

SHERIDAN: Debt. Company. A game. A club.

THURLOW: So, your support is growing.

SHERIDAN: Yes. The next vote will be close. Well?

THURLOW: I am not ready yet.

*The Palace has been closed for the winter so the furniture is under
dustsheets, the chandelier bagged, the rooms echoing and empty. The
party from Windsor comes down the stairs huddled in rugs, scarves
and overcoats, and carrying lanterns.* PAPANDIEK *wheels the* KING
in the chair, trundling it heavily down the stairs.

BRAUN: (*Sarcastically*) Sharp! Sharp! The King! The King!

KING: Not here. Not here. She is not here. What have you done
with her? She will be at Kew, you said.

WILLIS: It is not time. You are not fit to meet her yet.

KING: It was a lie! Not fit? You are an ordained minister, and
you told me a lie. Well, that lie, sir, will have you out of a
living. That lie will have you out of that famous farm of
yours, and loose your tame lunatics across Lincolnshire.
Liar! Liar!

WILLIS: Hush, sir. Her Majesty is here at Kew, and when you
learn to conduct yourself properly you shall see her.

KING: Mendacious old fool.

BRAUN: Cheer up, Georgie my old love.

KING: You rascal.

BRAUN: God, how he stinks.

KING: You slackarsed drizzle-prick. And you, you
sanctimonious piss-hole.

(WILLIS *motions for the clamps to be fastened and the* KING
restrained.)

WILLIS: I've had enough of this foolishness. Come to your
senses, sir.

KING: I can't come to my senses. I have to go to them, and I
cannot go to them because I am fastened here.

WILLIS: Now that we are safely in our new abode, shall we give
thanks? Let us pray.

KING: How can I? I cannot put my hands together.

WILLIS: Prayer is an attitude of the soul.

KING: Bollocks. You have to put your hands together or it
doesn't signify.

(*The* PAGES *sink wearily to their knees.*)

WILLIS: O God, who knowest us to be set in the midst of great

64

dangers that by reason of the frailty of our nature we cannot
always stand upright . . .

KING: Yes. And why? Liar.

WILLIS: . . . Grant to us such strength and protection as may
support us in all dangers and carry us through all
temptations, through Jesus Christ our Lord.

KING: Amen. Liar.

(*During the prayer we see* PITT *come down the stairs, out of sight
of the* KING.)

PITT: Amen.

(WILLIS *draws aside to speak to* PITT, *still keeping him out of
the* KING's *eyeline.*)

WILLIS: I was not expecting you, sir.

PITT: Why? It's Tuesday, my customary day.

WILLIS: It's Christmas Day.

PITT: Is it? It's all one to me. Handier, Kew.

WILLIS: Colder.

PITT: It's the summer palace.

WILLIS: Summer palaces, winter palaces . . . I am not up in such
matters. But I would have protested had I known. Sweats
and fevers in such a cold place will do him no good. It is a
tomb. I wonder the Prince of Wales does not appreciate that.

(PITT *says nothing, though it is plain the* PRINCE *appreciated it
only too well.* PAPANDIEK *is sitting hunched up by the* KING's
chair so that the two of them look like Lear and his Fool. PITT
regards them.)

PITT: I used to sit with my father too. Hours at a time. He would
not speak. When he was well he would read Shakespeare to
the family. When it came to the comic parts he handed the
book to me.

WILLIS: I have never read Shakespeare.

(PITT *looks with the nearest he comes to surprise.*)
I am a clergyman.

PITT: Your Majesty.

KING: Mr Pitt? Mr Pitt. I have something to say . . . No, no. Let
me up . . . let me up . . . from this . . . article for sitting in.
Let . . . me . . . up. I see my ministers vertical . . . eye to eye
two eye.

PITT: He is only trying to stand. Your Majesty is only trying to stand. Please sit, sir.

KING: No, no. (*He goes on struggling.*)

PAPANDIEK: Sir?

WILLIS: Very well.

(*The pages release the* KING *and he struggles to his feet.*)

KING: Mr Pitt . . . It is Mr Pitt, isn't it?

PITT: It is, sir.

KING: I have to be careful because I have all the state secrets. They listen, you know. (*To the pages*) Shoo, shoo. The parson particularly. Get away, you old goat. Go back to Lincolnshire. My son . . . my son comes and looks at me. Spies on me through the door. I've heard him laughing.

PITT: No, sir.

KING: Oh yes, sir. There was something else I wanted to tell you. Oh yes. They have killed the Queen. Did you know that?

PITT: No, sir.

KING: You keep saying 'No, sir'. *Yes, sir.* You do not know the world, Mr Pitt. I am sad about the Queen. Very sad. We were very happy. Are you cold?

PITT: It is chilly, sir.

KING: Not for me. I make the weather by means of mental powers . . . (*To* WILLIS) You know nothing. What do you know, you provincial fool? (*From being weepy he is suddenly cheerful.*) It's not too bad about the Queen, because I was actually never married to her. I was married to the tall one. Elizabeth. The old fool doesn't know it, but she's my real wife. The Queen's a good woman, but she's not a patch on Lady Pembroke.

WILLIS: Leave that, sir. Leave it.

KING: No, no. Leave us.

(*It is always the* KING's *sexual improprieties that galvanize* WILLIS *and he signals to the* PAGES *to fetch the straitwaistcoat, which is kept on a stand always ready. The* PAGES *hurriedly fasten him in, and he scarcely protests.*)

This is government. This is affairs of state.

WILLIS: It is nothing of the sort. It is filth.

KING: See, Mr Pitt. They fling me about like a sack of barley.

PITT: I will leave you, sir.

KING: (*With sudden authority*) No, you will not. I have not said you could. You do not leave the King until you are dismissed.

WILLIS: Mr Pitt may go. I say he may.
(*This breach of etiquette is about as big an affront to* PITT *as it is to the* KING, *and* PITT *swallows it with difficulty. The* PAGES *note it, too.*)

KING: I dismiss you. That is why you can go. But it is my say-so. Not his. Not his, Mr Pitt. Mine, do you hear? Dism-dismiss . . . miss . . . miss.
(PITT *moves out of the* KING's *restricted eyeline.*)

PITT: Dr Willis. I came hoping for some alteration. What am I to tell Parliament? It is over a month since you took charge of His Majesty, and I can detect no improvement.

WILLIS: It is there, I assure you.

PITT: He is different, certainly, but no better. Is there no other treatment? Is it . . . is it rigorous enough?

WILLIS: Sir?

PITT: You assured me you could cure him.

WILLIS: I can. I can.

PITT: Well, you had better hurry, because soon it will be too late.
(*Going.*)

KING: (*Shouting out*) Mr Pitt. Do nothing, Mr Pitt. Not Fox. I am not mad, Mr Pitt. Your father was mad. I saw him. I saw your father. He wasn't like me. You may go, Mr Pitt. I give you leave.
(PITT *goes.* WILLIS *comes and stands looking thoughtfully at the* KING *who chunters to himself but only half heard.*)
Whatever I think, the bells ring it, the dogs bark it, the birds sing it, the walls hear it. There are persons hiding in the walls, hiding in it now. They make me think thoughts I would not think, would not dream of thinking, would not think of dreaming, put them there, tormenting me, influencing my body, speaking the thought language . . .

WILLIS: Fetch Greville and Fitzroy, and the other page – where is he?
(PAPANDIEK *goes.*)

BRAUN: Fortnum, sir? He has left, sir. Said it was too much like work, sir. Gone to start a provision merchant's in Piccadilly, sir.

(PAPANDIEK *returns with* FITZROY *and* GREVILLE. WILLIS *motions all of them to line up in front of the* KING.)

WILLIS: I wish to remind Your Majesty, in the presence of your attendants, of your contract.

KING: What contract? There is no contract. I am King of England. I signed no contract . . . but I am contracted. I am shrunk. I signed no contract but I am not as majestic as I deserve by reason of damage sustained, whereby my right to be free was abstracted and constrained and I was locked up in this cage-weather and hear myself constantly promenaded in your figures of speech . . .

WILLIS: . . . Namely, if the King indulges in meaningless discourse, he will be restrained. If he struggles or strikes his attendants, he will be restrained. But if he indulges in filth or obscene talk, makes improper allegations aganst the Queen and Dr Willis . . . or entertains lascivious thoughts about Lady Pembroke, or any lady, then this is what you must do.

(WILLIS *suddenly gags the* KING *in full flow*.)

GREVILLE: No!

FITZROY: I will do no such thing.

PAPANDIEK: Nor me.

WILLIS: You will do it, because there is no more disrespect in it than turning off a tap. If this putrid discourse eased the King's mind of its poisons, then no, one would not turn it off. But it is not like that. All men, even ministers of religion, nurture such thoughts, but they do not infect our talk, because discretion and decorum filter them out. It is that filter His Majesty refuses to operate, must learn to operate again. And until he does . . . and we must hope, Your Majesty, it is *soon* . . .

(WILLIS *is interrupted by the arrival of* WARREN *and* PEPYS *dressed for a masquerade*.)

WARREN: All assembled? Splendid. Bidden to a seasonal gathering at Chiswick, Pepys and I thought to combine business with pleasure.

(PEPYS *makes a bee-line for the bedpan as usual*.)

I take it His Majesty has been talking again. For once, Willis, I think you are being very sensible.

WILLIS: Here is the bulletin.

(WARREN *looks it over.*)

PEPYS: No mention of the stool again, I suppose?

WARREN: Oh, the stool, the stool. My dear Pepys. The persistent excellence of the stool has been one of this disease's most tedious features. When will you get it into your mind that one can produce a copious, regular and exquisitely turned evacuation every day of the week, and still be a stranger to reason?

PEPYS: Nature provides us with these clues. We neglect them at our peril.

WARREN: Yes. Like the pulse . . . 'Less regular than one has known it on some occasions, more regular than on others.' And you say here he has been talking less. So why is he gagged?

WILLIS: Lasciviousness. But there has been some coherent conversation.

WARREN: Before witnesses?

WILLIS: Do you doubt my word, sir? I am a minister of religion.

WARREN: So was Caiaphas.

(WARREN *examines the* KING's *head.*)

These have healed up nicely. Which won't do at all. The wounds must be kept open, or the poisons will not flow. Blister him today and again tomorrow. And a very merry Christmas to you all.

PEPYS: Merry Christmas.

(*Hearing about the blistering the* KING *begins to struggle and moan through the gag as* PAPANDIEK *wheels him away.*)

WESTMINSTER

BURKE *begins his speech in a spotlight, then the wall splits again, revealing the Speaker's chair, etc., and he finishes his speech at the Despatch Box, though as always he has to raise his voice to make himself heard above the groans and catcalls that almost always accompanied his speeches (including those which have commended him to posterity as a great orator).*

SPEAKER: Mr Burke.

BURKE: In England we have not yet been completely embowelled of our natural entrails. We preserve real hearts of flesh and blood beating in our bosoms. We fear God. We look up with awe to kings, with affection to parliaments, with duty to magistrates, with reverence to priests and respect to the nobility. How much more terrible it is for every man of feeling among us to see this turn of events . . . the monarch smitten by the hand of omnipotence . . . a mind robbed of its understanding, a discourse deprived of moral rectitude. Should this frail and piteous wreck of a man govern this nation? Can he do so? I say, No! Let us look to the hope of this House, our Prince.

(*Shouts of* 'No, no!')

(*A government spokesman now speaks in dumbshow as* PITT *and* DUNDAS *come in, followed by* WILLIS.)

PITT: No, no. This will not do. This is practically the worst bulletin yet. I go into the House with this, we shall lose the vote outright.

(PITT *stands aside and starts drinking.*)

WILLIS: The bulletin is a joint production. As you know, some of the crew are pulling for the other shore.

DUNDAS: Then rewrite it.

WILLIS: Can I do that?

PITT: Of course, man. Show him, show him.

DUNDAS: You must. Here. Quick. Tone it down.

(DUNDAS *hands* WILLIS *a pen and he starts to re-draft the bulletin,* PITT *with his back to the pair of them. It is a case of* DUNDAS *doing* PITT'*s dirty work for him, the Prime Minister careful not to soil his hands.*)

DUNDAS: As it's written here it plays straight into Fox's hands. The vote is going to be close, closer than last time. We need some evidence of improvement to rally our supporters, to make the managers' task easier.

WILLIS: What managers?

PITT: The managers in the House, man.

DUNDAS: It need be no more than a night well spent. Does he still play the harpsichord?

WILLIS: Only a few bars.

DUNDAS: Then write it, man, write it. Anything that even abuts on normality. Is he still talking?

WILLIS: Less. But with no less filth and obscenity.

DUNDAS: Leave that, then.

(PITT *reads over the bulletin.*)

PITT: Yes, this is better. (*He exits.*)

DUNDAS: How is His Majesty . . . truthfully?

WILLIS: I need time.

(*The parliamentary debate takes place upstage centre while downstage left we see the* KING *in the restraining chair being treated by the London doctors, and* WILLIS *downstage right watching the activities of his colleagues without enthusiasm.*)

SPEAKER: Order, order. Mr Sheridan.

SHERIDAN: Mr Pitt brandishes an optimistic bulletin on His Majesty's health. It occurs to some of us on this side of the House that we always get these optimistic bulletins when this matter comes to a vote.

SPEAKER: Mr Pitt.

PITT: Mr Speaker, that is an outrageous suggestion.

SPEAKER: Mr Fox.

FOX: The matter at issue is not about the pitiful condition of the King. It is about the right of the Prince of Wales to govern this kingdom.

(*Shouts of* 'No, no'.)

PITT: The royal authority is not the Prince of Wales's by right. It belongs to Parliament. It is conferred by right of this House.

FOX: The King's illness is a civil death.

(*Shouts of* 'Oh'.)

The Prince of Wales has as clear and express a right to assume the reins of government as he would have were His Majesty laid in the grave.

(*Shouts of* 'Shame, shame'.)

PITT: But only if that right is confirmed by Parliament whose champion the honourable gentleman has always been.

Mr Fox claims to be a Whig. The speech he has just made

will un-Whig him for the rest of his life.

('Hear, hear', *etc*.)

FOX: The rest of my life is my own concern. I put the question again: when are we going to see the Bill appointing the Prince Regent?

(*Shouts of* 'When? When? When?')

PITT: In due course.

(*More uproar*.)

FOX: When?

(*Other shouts of* 'When?')

PITT: (*Losing control*) It is still being drafted.

(*More uproar*.)

Soon.

SPEAKER: Order, order.

WESTMINSTER

THURLOW: The Bill is ready. God's teeth, it has been ready for weeks, except that you keep wanting more restraints on the Prince. And they're a waste of time. This Government may tie his hands, the next will untie them.

(DUNDAS *comes in*.)

PITT: Well?

DUNDAS: We have the majority. Of ten.

THURLOW: Ten. That won't last long. You've lost the battle. You must present the Bill. The Prince must be made Regent. (*Cheerfully*) These things happen. The King is not going to recover.

DUNDAS: Not in time, certainly. And once the Prince of Wales is in charge we shall never know if he has recovered or not.

THURLOW: Why's that?

PITT: Because the Regent will mew him up in some Windsor boccado and mad or sane he will never be seen again.

THURLOW: You have been reading too many novels.

PITT: (*Taking the Bill*) Very well. I will present the Bill next week.

THURLOW: That's right. Get it over with. Get it over with. All

72

this excitement isn't good for me. I am sure my pulse has
gone up again. (*A* FOOTMAN *has entered.*) Yes, what is it?

FOOTMAN: Your hat, my Lord. Your Lordship left it in the
apartment of the Prince of Wales.

THURLOW: No. Not my hat. Take it away. Doesn't fit even.

FOOTMAN: Your name, sir. Your coat of arms.

THURLOW: So it is. Odd. Wonder how it got there. Still. Better
put it on, dammit, lest I lose it again. Ha! So. Good
afternoon, gentlemen.

PITT: Lord Chancellor.

(THURLOW *exits.*)

DUNDAS: How long has he been hanging his hat there?

PITT: I don't know. But why not? He has his reputation to
consider, after all. He has never been on the losing side yet.

WINDSOR

The KING, *sitting in the restraining chair, is playing cards with*
GREVILLE *and* PAPANDIEK, *the* KING *in nightgown and nightcap,*
GREVILLE *and* PAPANDIEK *both in their shirtsleeves and*
PAPANDIEK *without his wig.* FITZROY *is in attendance correctly*
attired and correctly behaved, and taking no part in the proceedings.
WILLIS, *as always, is in attendance.* BAKER *is just taking his leave of*
the KING.

KING:
GREVILLE: } Snap!

KING: Oh, by the way, Baker . . . One last thing . . .

BAKER: Sir?

KING: I have a little job for you. A secret mission.

BAKER: Yes, sir?

KING: I want you to hand over Gibraltar to Spain and see if you
can get Minorca in return. Do you think you could do that?

BAKER: I'm a physician, sir.

KING: Then you should have no difficulty. Good afternoon. My
go, is it?

(BAKER *shakes his head at* WILLIS *and goes out.*)

WILLIS: I have been watching you for a while, sir.

73

KING: ⎫
PAPANDIEK: ⎬ Snap!

KING: So you should. That's what they pay you for.

WILLIS: I have been watching you, but with a new eye.

KING: A new eye? Dear me. A new eye. And what does this new
    eye spy?

WILLIS: The nonsense that you talk is no longer helpless
    nonsense. Your improprieties are deliberate, sir, intentional.
    You enjoy them. They are uttered knowing you have the
    licence of a disturbed mind.

KING: I am the King. I say what I want.

ALL: Snip, snap, snorum.

WILLIS: You are playing a game, sir.

KING: I know. Snap.

WILLIS: No, sir, not snap. (*He snatches up the cards and stops the
    game.* FITZROY *hustles* GREVILLE *and* PAPANDIEK *from the
    table.*) You are playing a game with me, sir. Well, enough of
    it. If you choose you can behave.
    (*The* KING *tauntingly puts his feet on the table.* WILLIS *fixes him
    with his gaze and somewhat shamefacedly the* KING *removes
    them.*)
    Tell me the names of your children.

KING: Can't. Don't speak French.

WILLIS: *Sir.*

KING: Frederick, William, Charlotte, Edward, Augusta,
    Elizabeth, Earnest, Augustus, Adolphus, Mary, Sophia, my
    little Octavius, gone to his grave at four years old. Alfred –
    another dead one, Amelia.

WILLIS: No, you've missed one out.

KING: Don't be a devil, sir.

WILLIS: The Prince of Wales, say it, sir.

KING: (*Quietly*) George.

WILLIS: Say it.

KING: (*Louder*) George.

WILLIS: Good. And now the colonies.

KING: No. No. Do not look at me, sir.

WILLIS: Massachusetts . . .

KING: Don't be a devil.

74

WILLIS: Maine, Maryland, Virginia, Pennsylvania,
Connecticut . . .

KING: You do not cow me. I am not one of your Lincolnshire
lunatics. I am urban, metropolitan and royal, and not to be
stared down by the hard gaze of some provincial parson . . .
(*He begins to stutter and shake and* WILLIS *beckons*
PAPANDIEK *to strap him in the chair.*)
Take your hands off me, you clumsy fool.

PAPANDIEK: (*Shocked*) Sir!

KING: Oaf.

PAPANDIEK: Yes, sir.

KING: No, sir.
(*He strikes* PAPANDIEK, *who falls, hitting his head hard on the
floor.*)

BRAUN: The Queen, the Queen!

FITZROY: (*To the* PAGES) Man the door.

WILLIS: No!

FITZROY: His Majesty is not permitted to see the Queen by order
of the Prince.

WILLIS: Admit her. Now sir. You have a visitor. I will be
watching you, sir. Keep it under, sir. Keep it under.
(*The* QUEEN *comes in. The* KING *turns his head away and will
not look at her.*)

QUEEN: Your Majesty. Have you nothing to say to me, sir?

KING: (*Sotto voce*) Say, madam? What is there to say? We were
married for twenty-eight years, never separated even for a
day, then you abandon me to my tormentors. Ingratitude,
that is what I say.
(*Loudly, so that* WILLIS *can hear*) It does me good to see you,
my dear.

QUEEN: The doctor said it was for your good, sir.

KING: (*Sotto voce*) My good? What do they know of my good?
(*Loudly*) This is a good little woman. The best. (*Sotto voce*)
He's an old fool. I can't see what you see in him. (*Starts
talking quickly in German*) Du blöde Kuh. Er ist nur ein
Pfarrer. Du bist eine Hure und eine Schlampe.

WILLIS: What is His Majesty saying?

KING: Oh, do they not speak German in Lincolnshire then? *Du*

75

bist nicht hübsch. Elizabeth ist viel hübscher als du. Ich werde
mit ihr schlafen. Ich werde nicht mit dir schlafen bis
siebzehnhundert drei and neunzig . . .

QUEEN: He is saying he does not like me. There is someone else
he prefers. And I shall not share his bed again until . . . 1793
. . . *(She weeps.)*

(The KING *goes on jabbering . . .)*

KING: *. . . weil ihre titten grosser als deiner sind . . .*

QUEEN: . . . because . . .

KING: *Sie sind wie zwei reifen Melonon . . .*

WILLIS: Because what? Filth? Obscenities?

KING: *Ich möchte sie küssen . . .*

(The QUEEN *nods tearfully.)*

WILLIS: I see you, sir.

*(*WILLIS *dangles the gag in front of the* KING *but the* QUEEN
pushes him away.)

QUEEN: Go away, sir. I have something to say to His Majesty
alone. Alone. George. It is possible they will not permit me
to see you again. There is a Bill prepared to make the son
Regent. Do you understand me? To rule in your place.

KING: Regent? The fat one? No. No. This cannot be.

FITZROY: Madam, please. His Majesty has not been told about
the Bill.

QUEEN: Sir, he must be told.

KING: Regent?

QUEEN: Yes, and not only Regent. Because if the Bill passes, and
they say it will pass, then we shall be separated, you and I,
for good.

KING: For good. No, it is not good. No. I told Mr Pitt . . .

QUEEN: No, George. Not Mr Pitt. Not any more. It will be
Mr Fox.

KING: Fox?

QUEEN: The son and Mr Fox. We shall not see each other again.
George. Do you understand me?

KING: No, no. No. Oh.

(The KING *begins to shake and judder and try to break free from*
his chair. He stamps his feet and, the QUEEN *trying to stop him,*
clasps his legs, shouting above the din.)

QUEEN: George! George!

WILLIS: You must leave, madam.

FITZROY: Come away, madam, come away.

KING: No. No.

(FITZROY *and* WILLIS *drag her off the* KING, *and* WILLIS *escorts her from the room.*)

No. Do not leave me. Do not leave me. My skin burns like it used to. Fetch the waistcoat. (*He begins to rave.*) Oh, but the son. The father pushed aside, put out, put away. Ruled out. The father not dead even.

Fetch the waistcoat. Fetch it.

(PAPANDIEK *looks for permission to* GREVILLE *who nods, so fetches it for the* KING, *who puts it on.*)

Fasten it.

Fasten it.

(WILLIS *returns, as the* KING *stands in front of* GREVILLE, *then* PAPANDIEK, *wanting their help in fastening it.*)

Greville.

Arthur.

Braun.

WILLIS: No. Leave it.

KING: But it frets my guts out like it used to.

WILLIS: You are the master now. Time was when you could not be induced to wear it. Now you must cast it off.

KING: Greville, Arthur, Fitzroy . . . It is stronger than I am.

WILLIS: Control it, sir. Control it. Fight it, sir. Fight it.

(*The* KING *struggles and fights, almost as if he were having a fit. Gradually the fit passes, and the* KING *droops exhausted and the waistcoat falls from him.*)

Now, sir. Call your dissipated spirits home.

(*The* KING *picks up the waistcoat and hands it to* BRAUN *then takes* WILLIS'*s hand and kisses it.*)

KING: Oh, thank you, sir.

WILLIS: Now there is another whom you have offended, whom you struck just now.

KING: Papandiek.

WILLIS: You must ask his forgiveness.

PAPANDIEK: No.

77

GREVILLE: His Majesty must not.

KING: Forgive me. Give me your pardon.

(PAPANDIEK *kisses the* KING'*s hand*.)

WILLIS: No.

GREVILLE: This is his *page*.

WILLIS: No matter. He must be broken as a horse is broken.

(*The* KING *takes* PAPANDIEK'*s hand*.)

KING: Arthur . . .

(*He kneels before* PAPANDIEK *and kisses his hand*.)

CARLTON HOUSE

FITZROY *steps from one scene to the next and also kneels, but to the*
PRINCE OF WALES.

PRINCE OF WALES: This time tomorrow, Fitzroy, we shall be
Regent and you will be our Master of the Horse, so we give
you leave now to kiss our hand by way of acceptance.

(FITZROY *kisses his hand*.)

SHERIDAN: As soon as the Bill is passed Your Royal Highness
should dismiss from any public office all who have
supported Pitt, and replace them with our own people. By
my calculations that will give us a regular majority of 150 at
the very least.

PRINCE OF WALES: Quite comfortable.

DUKE OF YORK: Nothing for me, I suppose?

PRINCE OF WALES: I've just made you Colonel of the Coldstreams.

DUKE OF YORK: Sorry. So you have. I discovered the other day that
I'm a Fellow of the Royal Society. Amazing what one is really.

PRINCE OF WALES: So far as concerns our royal invalid, this
Willis should be packed off back to Lincolnshire at once
and Warren knighted and put in sole charge.

WARREN: Sir.

PRINCE OF WALES: Though since he is plainly in decline, you
won't need to be in daily attendance. After all, a watched
pot never boils. Meanwhile, we are thinking of having a
Regency medal minted, and that will need to be designed,
and I'm wondering about another throne. Decisions,

decisions. Government, so exhausting.

BURKE: Could I show your Royal Highness a list of measures we might consider putting before Parliament . . .

PRINCE OF WALES: Not now. Charles, I expected you to be more cheerful. You're on the brink of office, after all.

FOX: I am contemplating my responsibilities, sir.

PRINCE OF WALES: Don't. Just think of your debts being paid. All our debts being paid. I shall do things differently from my father. To me style is the thing. The King has never had any style. From now on, style is going to be everything.

SHERIDAN: It's to be hoped that it is. Then we can get on with the boring business of government.

(BURKE *presses his list of proposals once more on the* PRINCE.)

BURKE: Your Royal Highness . . .

(*The* PRINCE *snatches the list from* BURKE *and screws it up.*)

PRINCE OF WALES: We do need Burke? Yes? So tiring.

(PRINCE OF WALES, DUKE OF YORK *and* WARREN *go.*)

BURKE: This list of proposals that I wanted to put to His Royal Highness . . .

(SHERIDAN *takes the list.*)

SHERIDAN: Abolition of the slave trade . . . parliamentary reform. These will be as unwelcome to the Prince as they would be to his father.

BURKE: In which case the Prince must be made to realize that the Crown, be it King or Regent, is subject to Parliament, and that . . .

FOX: No, no. Sheridan is right. We must not spit on our luck. These will have to wait, my dear. Let us come in first. Then in due course we will put paid to Mr Pitt and his kitchen principles. I will show this counting-house clerk that the nation is not simply a household. Let a housewife be thrifty, modest and shy – government is bold, restless and prodigal. It is prodigious in its expenditure, recalcitrant in its debts, lofty in its assumptions. It is not all thrift. Popular government has nothing to do with thrift.

SHERIDAN: It hasn't much to do with popularity, either.

FOX: That is because we have never had time – now we shall be in office for ten years at the very least . . . What's up?

SHERIDAN: Something is not right. The Prince is about to be made Regent. The Government is on its last legs. We have won. Where is Thurlow?

WINDSOR

The KING *is laid on his couch, reading Shakespeare.* WILLIS *and* GREVILLE *are reading parts.*

WILLIS: 'Be better suited;
    These weeds are memories of those worser hours.'
KING: 'I prithee put them off.' Go on, go on.
WILLIS: 'I prithee put them off.'
KING: 'How does the King?'
WILLIS: 'How does the King?'
PAPANDIEK: Lord Thurlow, Your Majesty.
KING: Ah, Thurlow. The very man.
THURLOW: Your Majesty.
KING: We are reading a spot of Shakespeare. Willis, give him the book, or share.
THURLOW: (*Sotto voce to* WILLIS) *King Lear?* Is that wise?
KING: Willis chose it. Doctor's orders.
WILLIS: I'd no idea what it was about.
KING: It's my story. Now. I'm asleep apparently, and Cordelia comes in and asks the Doctor – that's Greville – how I am, you see. Off we go.
THURLOW: Who's Cordelia?
KING: You are. Well, Willis can't do it. He's hopeless. Willis. Go down there, and watch. Right then, off we go.
THURLOW: (*As Cordelia*) 'O you kind gods
    Cure this great breach in his abused nature.
    Th'untuned and jarring senses, O wind up,
    Of this child-changed father.'
KING: That's very good. 'Child-changed father''s very good. Go on, Greville, you now.
GREVILLE: (*As Doctor*) 'He hath slept long, be by, good madam,
    when we do awaken him.
    I doubt not of his temperance.'

THURLOW: 'O my dear father! Restoration hang
        Thy medicine on my lips, and let this . . . kiss
    (THURLOW *looks alarmed*.)
        Repair those violent harms that my two sisters
        Have in thy reverence made.'
KING: Well, kiss me, man. Come on, come on. It's Shakespeare.
    (THURLOW *goes for the* KING'*s hand*.)
KING: No, no. Here, man. Here. (*Gives him his cheek*.) Push off
    now. This is where the King awakens.
THURLOW: 'How does my royal lord? How fares Your Majesty?'
KING: (*As Lear*) 'You do me wrong to take me out o' th' grave.
        Thou art a soul in bliss, but I am bound
        Upon a wheel of fire, that mine own tears
        Do scald like molten lead. (Oh, it's so true!)
        Pray do not mock me.
        I am a very foolish, fond old man.
    (*The* KING *clasps* THURLOW.)
        And to deal plainly
        I fear I am not in my perfect mind.
        Do not laugh at me.
        For as I am a man, I think this lady
        To be my child Cordelia.'
THURLOW: (*Much affected*) 'And so I am. I am.'
GREVILLE: 'Be comforted good madam, the great rage
        You see is killed in him;
        Desire him to go in, trouble him no more
        Till further settling.'
THURLOW: 'Will't please your Highness walk?'
    (*The* KING *stands, first as Lear, then as himself*.)
KING: There.
WILLIS: So is that the end?
KING: No, no . . . Cordelia – that's Thurlow – dies. Hanged. And
    the shock of it kills the King. So they all die. It's a tragedy.
THURLOW: (*Blowing his nose*) Very affecting.
KING: It's the way I play it. Willis murders it.
THURLOW: Your Majesty seems more yourself.
KING: Do I? Yes, I do. I have always been myself even when I
    was ill. Only now I seem myself. That's the important thing.

I have remembered how to seem. What, what?

GREVILLE: What did Your Majesty say?

KING: What? I didn't say anything. Besides, Greville, you're not
supposed to ask the King questions, you should know that.
What, what? Bear with me, Thurlow. (*He sees the curtain,
takes hold of it and does an old ham's curtain call.*) 'Pray you
now forget and forgive; I am old and foolish.' Awfully good
stuff, isn't it?

(*The* KING *and* THURLOW *go off.*)

WILLIS: I will write to Mr Pitt straightaway. And send for
Warren and Baker. They must see the King at once.

(WILLIS *and* GREVILLE *rush off, as* BRAUN *and* PAPANDIEK
come on from opposite sides, each with a glass chamber pot.)

BRAUN: Look at his piss. We're back to lemonade.

PAPANDIEK: Mine isn't. It's still a bit inky.

BRAUN: But that's yesterday's. This is today's. Piss the Elder!
Piss the Younger!

WESTMINSTER

PITT *and* DUNDAS.

PITT: Wreckers, destroyers. Thinkers. The nation is neatly
governed, farming improves, manufacturing prospers, and
Fox and his feckless friends cannot wait to ruin it all.

DUNDAS: Another letter from Willis.

(*He is reading it.*)

PITT: The King is much better?

DUNDAS: Yes.

PITT: When did Willis say otherwise? He has been pretending the
King is better for months. I never believed him but
Parliament did. Now Parliament does not believe him either,
and so the Bill of Regency will pass. By how many?

DUNDAS: Oh, forty or fifty. I've given up counting. They're all
running for cover. William! A smile!

PITT: At least it will clear my desk. It is the King one should pity.
Declared mad, he will stay mad. His son would be a fool to
have it otherwise. The asylums of this country are full of the

sound-in-mind disinherited by the out-of-pocket.

DUNDAS: Even if he did recover and found Fox his minister, he would go mad all over again.

PITT: But how they will spend! All the money I have saved. All the waste I have eradicated. Gone. Money. That is the whole secret of government. Funds. Economy. The elimination of waste. I know that I can save this country and no one else can, but I needed five more years. Instead of which I must go back to the Bar.

DUNDAS: Come, that's not true. The City has offered to pay your debts and give you an income.

PITT: To do what? Sit on the back benches and carp. There is no dignity in that. No. I will never consider taking any post but the first.

(*Enter* THURLOW.)

FOOTMAN: The Lord Chancellor.

PITT: This is an unexpected pleasure, Lord Chancellor. We see you so seldom nowadays. Your visits are always a joy.

THURLOW: Leave all that, damn it. I've been with His Majesty and have had two hours' uninterrupted conversation with him.

DUNDAS: Oh God, you mean he's talking again?

THURLOW: No, dammit. Well, yes. But not fifty to the dozen, and not nonsense either. He's actually a damned clever fellow. Had me reading Shakespeare. Have you read *King Lear*? Tragic story. Of course, if that fool of a messenger had just got that little bit more of a move on, Cordelia wouldn't have been hanged, Lear wouldn't have died, and it would all have ended happily . . . which I think would have made a much better ending. Because as it is, it's so damned tragic . . .

DUNDAS: Lord Chancellor . . .

THURLOW: The point is, the King is better.

PITT: Better than he was?

THURLOW: No. Better in every respect. Improved out of all measure. The 'what what' is back. The 'hey hey'. He is his old self.

(PITT *and* DUNDAS *are ready to rush off when* THURLOW *stops them.*)

That having been said, gentlemen, I would like to explain

again that my aim as Lord Chancellor throughout this whole unfortunate episode has been to withdraw myself, so far as I could, from any allegiance to party or faction . . .

PITT: Of course.

(PITT *and* DUNDAS *go as the acoustic changes to Parliament.*)

THURLOW: There must be continuity, consistency. I was holding the scales . . .

VOICE: Sitting on the fence.

THURLOW: That is unkind. When I forsake my King in the hour of his distress may my God forsake me. But next to the King I reverence the Prince of Wales, nor do I believe there is a man in this assembly who entertains a higher opinion of his heart and head than I do, and though I rejoice that the Bill of Regency has proved unnecessary, I pray that one day the crown may in succession sit upon the Prince's brow as undisturbed and as ornamental as it now sits upon that of his father. His Majesty has been restored to us. God – and I say this with all my heart and a clear conscience – God save the King.

WINDSOR

The concluding part of Zadok the Priest (*'God save the King, God save the King, May the King live forever', etc.) as the full stage is revealed and the* KING, *wigged again and in his court uniform, awaits the arrival of the* QUEEN, *who comes in accompanied as ever by* LADY PEMBROKE. WILLIS *is in the background.*

GREVILLE: Her Majesty the Queen, Your Majesty.

(*They curtsey and* LADY PEMBROKE *withdraws as the* KING *embraces the* QUEEN *and sits her beside him.* GREVILLE, *having retired, now returns and whispers to the* KING.)

KING: The doctors? What do they want? I'm better, aren't I? What, what?

QUEEN: You are. You are.

WILLIS: Sir, may I make a suggestion? Why does Your Majesty not dismiss them?

KING: Yes, why do I not dis . . . (*Pause.*) Can I do that?

84

WILLIS: It is what Your Majesty would have done before your
   illness.
QUEEN: Do it, George.
GREVILLE: The physicians, Your Majesty.
   (*The doctors come in.*)
BAKER: (*Taking the* KING'*s pulse*) With Your Majesty's
   permission.
   (PEPYS *examines the bedpan.*)
WARREN: Did Your Majesty pass an untroubled night? Was there
   any sweating?
KING: I'm sorry. Did someone speak?
GREVILLE: Dr Warren enquired whether Your Majesty had
   passed a comfortable night, sir.
KING: The King passed an excellent night, but to quiz him on the
   matter is a gross impertinence. And Greville?
GREVILLE: Your Majesty?
KING: There was no sweating.
PEPYS: (*Who has found the chamber pot under the restraining chair.*)
   The stool is good. A model of its kind. May I congratulate
   Your Majesty on another splendid stool.
KING: (*Vehemently*) No, you may not.
PEPYS: (*Still not understanding*) Oh. Well, it is very good.
   (*He shows it to an equally furious* WARREN. *Pause.*)
QUEEN: Do it, George.
KING: Yes. Well, will there be anything more, gentlemen?
WARREN: Perhaps we might have a little general conversation
   with Your Majesty?
QUEEN: What about?
KING: Yes. What about?
WARREN: Oh . . . topics.
QUEEN: Do it, George.
KING: No. That will be all, gentlemen.
WARREN: All? All?
KING: Yes, all, you fashionable fraud. Go and blister some other
   blameless bugger, what what.
   (*The* KING *gets up and himself shows the door to the disconcerted
   doctors.*)
QUEEN: (*Clapping her hands*) Sir!

KING: And Baker?

BAKER: Sir?

KING: Backwards, Baker. Backwards.

(*The* KING *is delighted at his own boldness, kisses the* QUEEN *and picks her up and whirls her round.*)

WILLIS: Well done, sir. Full marks.

KING: Yes. And you can go too, Willis.

WILLIS: I don't think so, sir. Not quite yet.

KING: No? Horse not broken yet, is that it? But the day is coming, I promise. What? Lincolnshire shall see you soon. The wolds are agog.

FITZROY: Their Royal Highnesses are here, Your Majesty.

WILLIS: Your Majesty must not agitate yourself.

KING: I know that.

QUEEN: He knows that. Two hours late. It's done on purpose. He knows it was always his lateness drove you mad.

(*She claps her hand over her mouth.*)

KING: Never fear. I shall strike a note of reconciliation. Love, that is the keynote.

FITZROY: Their Royal Highnesses, Your Majesty.

(*The* PRINCE OF WALES *and the* DUKE OF YORK *come in.*)

DUKE OF YORK: Pa.

KING: You may kiss my hand. And your mother's.

DUKE OF YORK: Ma.

PRINCE OF WALES: How is Your Majesty?

KING: Fat lot you care.

QUEEN: Love, George.

KING: I am well, sir.

QUEEN: Though weary with waiting.

KING: Two hours! Two hours!

QUEEN: George. Love.

(*The* KING *controls himself.*)

He's still fat.

(*The waistcoat is still on its stand by the restraining chair.*)

KING: I see you are looking at my waistcoat, sir.

PRINCE OF WALES: No. No, sir. No.

KING: No no no, sir. You may, sir, you may, because it is the best friend I ever had. But I have the advantage of you, sir. I can

86

take off my waistcoat. This corpulence, sir. Fight it, sir. Fight it. You smile, sir.

PRINCE OF WALES: Only to see my father his old self, and in such good spirits, sir.

KING: Good or bad, I am in control of them, sir. When a man can control himself, sir, his spirits are immaterial. When a man cannot control himself he would do well to be sober, he would do well to be . . .

(WILLIS *coughs discreetly and the* KING *instantly recovers himself*.)

For the future, we must try to be more of a family. There are model farms now, model villages, even model factories. Well, we must be a model family for the nation to look to.

QUEEN: Yes. Try to be typical, Fred.

PRINCE OF WALES: But Pa, I want something to do.

KING: Do? Well, follow in my footsteps, that is what you should do, and forget all this furniture. Style never immortalized anybody. Off you go.

(*They go*.)

QUEEN: The oversized turbot. I rue the day he was born.

KING: Yes. He is a feckless, weak, irresolute, lying, contemptible wretch.

QUEEN: And he gambles too . . .

KING: But you are right. We must try not to dislike him.

FITZROY: Mr Pitt, Your Majesty.

KING: My dear.

QUEEN: Oh yes. *Männersache, ja?*

(*The* QUEEN *goes off and the* KING *starts where he left off six months before*.)

Married yet, Mr Pitt?

PITT: No, sir.

KING: Good God.

(*The* KING *is suddenly transfixed by the paper* PITT *has given him and runs to the restraining chair*.)

Fasten me in.

PAPANDIEK: Sir?

WILLIS: Sir, what is it?

KING: Is it any wonder a man goes mad? Doctors. Thirty guineas a visit? And travelling expenses. For six months of torture. They would make a man pay for his own execution. What? What?

WILLIS: Your Majesty must not get excited.

KING: Yes. I know. But we are about to see the back of 'must not' and renew our acquaintance with 'as His Majesty pleases'. But no bill for Willis. How much is he getting?

PITT: No fee, sir, but he has been promised an annuity.

KING: How much?

PITT: £1,000 a year, sir. He has done you some service, sir.

KING: No. It is Time that has done me the service.

(*The* KING *suddenly claps his hand over his mouth.*)

Basin! Basin!

(*The* KING *rushes off, followed by the* PAGES.)

WILLIS: I slipped two grains of tartar emetic into His Majesty's breakfast posset. One cannot be too careful.

PITT: What purpose does the vomiting serve?

WILLIS: The ostensible purpose is to reduce the burden on the organs of digestion, but what it also does is to remind His Majesty that he is not yet a well man, that he must tread warily . . .

PITT: And that he is still beholden to his doctor.

(WILLIS *leaves as the* KING *returns.*)

KING: They tell me that the vomiting will be the last symptom to go. It's odd that it still continues because I feel perfectly well. But you are too pale, Mr Pitt. You should ride, Mr Pitt. I rode nine hours a day, and shall again.

GREVILLE: Mr Ramsden Skrymshir, Your Majesty.

(RAMSDEN *comes in, alone this time but as genially vacant as ever.*)

KING: Another asking face. Sir. What is this? (*Looking at the paper* PITT *gives him*) Markets? I bet he don't know a pig from a goose.

PITT: No, sir. But his uncle is Member for Berkshire and has the nomination of three other seats in Hampshire.

(*The* KING *signs.*)

KING: I would have made a good Steward of the Market at Newbury. I would have done it very well. Counting the sheep.

Overlooking the cattle. (*He gives the warrant to* RAMSDEN.)
Happy man, Ramsden, happy man.
(*The* KING *offers his hand to be kissed but* RAMSDEN *shakes it heartily.* SIR BOOTHBY *suddenly materializes in the doorway.*)

SIR BOOTHBY: (*Hissing*) 'Your devoted servant, sir.'
(RAMSDEN *nods amiably, as if in agreement.*)

KING: Off you go, young man.
(RAMSDEN *heads for the door* (*and not backwards*), *but the* KING *stops him.*)

KING: And Ramsden, a little tip. The cow is the one with horns and the pig is the one with the little curly tail, what what. Do well, Ramsden, do well.
(SIR BOOTHBY's *arm comes out to yank the hapless* RAMSDEN *away.*)
Except that Ramsden will not do well. He will not even do. He will go away and nominate a deputy and the deputy will put in a substitute and the substitute find him a drudge, and the drudge will do the work. Or not. And so it is from top to bottom in England. But what of Europe, Mr Pitt? Nobody has talked of that yet.

PITT: Nothing of moment, sir. There have been some minor disturbances in Paris, and the mob broke open the Bastille.

KING: The Bastille? The terror is in the word. It is no different from the prison I have been in these last few months.

PITT: Mr Fox got very . . . inspired, but order seems to have been restored. I do not think we have much to fear from France this decade.

KING: We shall meet at the Thanksgiving Service in St Paul's. I must thank God for my recovery. And so must you, Mr Pitt. So must you. What, what. As for the future, Mr Pitt, you are not to disagree with me, on anything, what? My mind is not strong enough to stand it.
(*It should not be clear if the* KING *is serious or trying it on.*)

PITT: I will do my duty, sir.

KING: 'The oldest hath borne most. You that are young
        Shall never see so much nor live so long.'
(*As the* KING *leaves through one door,* BRAUN *and* PAPANDIEK *burst in through the other.*)

89

BRAUN: Sacked? Jesus!

PAPANDIEK: And me! I was His Majesty's devoted servant.

GREVILLE: Were you pages to the Czar or servants to the Sultan you would not have been dismissed. You would have had your throats cut.

BRAUN: Yes. And so would the doctors.

GREVILLE: Forget what you have seen. Majesty in its small clothes. Wipe it from your memory.

PAPANDIEK: He was ill. We knew that.

GREVILLE: Yes, and now he is well. Here.

(BRAUN *takes the money and strolls off.*)

PAPANDIEK: Sir, I am fond of His Majesty.

GREVILLE: You are not entitled to be. You are his servant. You will not be without employment. I hear your old colleague Fortnum has founded a grocery business. You could join him.

PAPANDIEK: Fortnum and *Papandiek*?

(*While no more unlikely a coupling than, say, Justerini and Brooks,* PAPANDIEK *sees no future in it, and takes the money and goes.*

FITZROY *has been observing these proceedings with his customary disdain.*)

FITZROY: You were kind to His Majesty during his illness, Greville.

GREVILLE: I did what I could, Captain Fitzroy.

FITZROY: Colonel Fitzroy. You did not know that? It seems unfair, I agree. But a word of advice. To be kind does not commend you to kings. They see it, as they see any flow of feeling, as a liberty. A blind eye will serve you better. And you will travel further.

FOOTMAN: Sharp! Sharp! The King! The King!

(*The* KING *is ready for bed when* LADY PEMBROKE *enters with her invariable candlestick. The* KING *waves away the footman. So they are alone.*)

KING: Hey, hey. Lady Pembroke.

LADY PEMBROKE: Your Majesty.

KING: Elizabeth.

LADY PEMBROKE: Sir.

KING: You know, Elizabeth. You are a model of English womanhood, what, what.

LADY PEMBROKE: I hope so, sir.

KING: Though there is what I would call the Upper Woman and the . . . the Lower Woman, hey, hey?

LADY PEMBROKE: Your Majesty must take care not to catch cold.

KING: Quite, yes, quite. When I was ill . . . Elizabeth . . . they tell me . . . I said . . . certain things, hey?

LADY PEMBROKE: It's possible, sir.

KING: These things I said, can you recollect any of them?

LADY PEMBROKE: I have no memory of them, sir.

KING: Well, perhaps I can refresh your memory because among the things I believe I suggested to you was that you and I might . . . that you and I had . . .

LADY PEMBROKE: It's possible that things were said then that in happier circumstances would not have been said.

KING: Said by both of us? Said by you and me, what, what?

LADY PEMBROKE: No, sir. Your Majesty was the persistent conversationalist.

KING: It's not so much what was said, as what was done, what. So did we . . . Did we ever . . .?

LADY PEMBROKE: Your Majesty?

KING: Did we ever forget ourselves utterly, because if we did forget ourselves I would so like to remember. What, what?

LADY PEMBROKE: No, sir. Your Majesty's behaviour throughout was impeccable. If I may say so, Your Majesty has always acted by me as the kindest brother as well as the most gracious of sovereigns.

KING: Have I? (*Sadly*) I am glad to hear it.

LADY PEMBROKE: Her Majesty is ready, sir.
  (*She conducts the* KING *in and then withdraws. The* QUEEN *is in bed, knitting as she was at the start of the play.*)

KING: My dear.

QUEEN: How is Your Majesty this evening, sir?

KING: Oh, better, madam. So much better. Better and better. Do not be nervous. I have missed you, madam.

QUEEN: Yes, sir.

KING: There is something about you . . .

QUEEN: (*Letting down her hair*) I am grey now, sir. Grey as an old mouse.

KING: Oh well. It is no matter.

QUEEN: I have lost what little share of beauty I once possessed.

KING: Still, you're a good little pudding.

QUEEN: When you were ill, it was said by some that had you led a . . . a normal life . . . it might not have happened.

KING: A normal life?

QUEEN: Other women, sir.

KING: Kicked over the traces, you mean, hey! No life is without its regrets. Yet none is without consolations. You are a good little woman, Mrs King. And we have been happy, have we not?

QUEEN: Yes, Mr King, we have.

KING: And shall be again. And shall be again.

(*The* KING *begins to stutter on the last phrase so that we are left with the sense that the future may not be quite as trouble-free as it appears. This is confirmed when a curtain is swiftly drawn across the scene and following it, keeping pace with it, comes a modern doctor:* DR IDA MACALPINE. *Following her come the three* PAGES, *a little nervous at suddenly finding themselves in the twentieth century.* GREVILLE *and* FITZROY *come on from the other side of the stage, though even a time-lurch of a couple of centuries does not manage to discompose* FITZROY.)

DR MACALPINE: He's better, of course, but he's not cured. And he's not going to be cured. Urine, young man. You were quite right.

FORTNUM: Blue?

BRAUN: Purple.

DR MACALPINE: Exactly. The colour of porphyry. Hence the name of the disease. I wrote a book about it.

(*She holds the book up. Before* PAPANDIEK *gets a chance to look at it,* FITZROY *comes up behind her and takes it.*)

FITZROY: 'Porphyria. George III was suffering from a metabolic disorder that produced chemical changes in the nervous system and symptoms similar to dementia and dermatitis.'

BRAUN: So was the old boy mad?

DR MACALPINE: Not at all. He just had all the symptoms of it.

FORTNUM: When was this book written?

DR MACALPINE: 1969.

PAPANDIEK: (*Looking at the book*) 'He has another attack in 1802 and finally takes leave of his senses in 1810, and dies deaf and blind in 1820.' Aw, the poor old sod.

GREVILLE: What about all the treatment?

DR MACALPINE: A waste of time. They'd have done better to leave him alone.

FITZROY: They're doctors. They're not paid to leave people alone.

(DR MACALPINE *goes off.*)

PAPANDIEK: Sir. If he wasn't mad but had all the symptoms, what's the difference?

BRAUN: It's nothing to be ashamed of then, is it?

PAPANDIEK: (*Humane to the last*) I thought it was nothing to be ashamed of anyway.

(*Sound of bells and* 'Sharp! Sharp! The King! The King! *The* PAGES *exeunt.*)

FITZROY: At least he's better off than the King of France. He's lost his head completely.

ST PAUL's

He pulls the curtain back to reveal the KING *and* QUEEN *in full state robes* (*a fond stage direction, as it turned out as there was no money left out of the National Theatre budget to run up some state robes so it was just their everyday royal togs*).

WILLIS: I shall be at the Cathedral, should the ceremony prove to be too great a burden for you, Your Majesty.

(*He has laid his hand on the* KING's *arm. The* KING *looks at it and* WILLIS *removes it.*)

KING: You may tell Dr Willis that the ceremony will not be such a burden as the want of ceremony has been. And do not look at me, sir. Presume not I am the thing I was. I am not the patient. Be off, sir. Back to your sheep and your pigs. The King is himself again.

(WILLIS *is escorted out as the* KING *and* QUEEN *go slowly up*

93

the steps, accompanied by Handel and attended by the company.
They are met at the door of St Paul's by the Archbishop of
Canterbury who blesses the newly recovered monarch, and the
KING *raises his hat to the crowds as the curtain falls.*)